# DYNAMO

Andy Dougan is a writer for the *Evening Times* and the author of six previous books; biographies of Martin Scorsese and Robert De Niro among them.

# DYNAMO

## DEFENDING THE HONOUR OF KIEV

Andy Dougan

FOURTH ESTATE • *London*

This paperback edition first published in 2002
First published in Great Britain in 2001 by
Fourth Estate
A Division of HarperCollins*Publishers*
77–85 Fulham Palace Road,
London W6 8JB
www.4thestate.co.uk

10  9  8  7  6  5  4  3  2  1

A catalogue record for this book is available from the
British Library

ISBN 1–84115–319–2

Typeset in Plantin by MATS, Southend-on-Sea, Essex

Printed in Great Britain by Clays Ltd, St Ives plc

*For Christine, Iain and Stuart*
*and dedicated to the bravery and heroism of the*
*men of FC Start*
*especially Kolya, Vanya, Sasha and Nikolai*

# ACKNOWLEDGEMENTS

This book has been a long time, almost three years, in the research and writing. Although mine were the fingers on the keys to put the words on the pages, there are a great many other people who were responsible for getting me to the stage where I could get this story down on paper.

There are specifically a number of people to whom I shall always be grateful and without whose efforts this book would not have been possible. Chief among them·is Vitaly Yerenkov whose tireless work on his fact-finding mission to Kiev and his follow-up investigations produced many invaluable documents and interviews, most of which form the basis for the factual background of this book. I am also grateful to Vitaly for his anecdotal and cultural insights into the lifestyle of the Ukrainian people. In Kiev I must also thank journalist and Dynamo Kiev fan Vitaly Borshchov, and Marina Shevchenko, of the National Museum of the Great Patriotic War. While we are dealing with those who provided material for the book I would like to thank Sergei Baltacha for sharing his memories of his own time defending the honour of Dynamo Kiev, and Phil Gordon for putting us in touch.

I am grateful also to Marc Reiper for sparing some time under difficult personal circumstances to try to offer some insights into the mind of the professional footballer, and also to Peter McLean for arranging our meeting.

My agent Jane Judd also deserves special mention for being so committed to the project. She was enthusiastic when I brought the project to her all those years ago and, whatever else occupied me in between times, she never let me forget the men of Dynamo Kiev. She showed the patience of Job through some excruciatingly bad early drafts and gently but firmly shepherded the book to the form you have before you now. It has been the single most satisfying experience of my writing career and I cannot thank her enough. My thanks also to Trevor Dolby at Orion who was one of the book's early supporters and, of course, to Clive Priddle at Fourth Estate who was finally willing to take a chance on it. Clive also showed extraordinary patience and insight during the editing process.

Writing is supposed to be a solitary pursuit. Tell that to my family and friends who have had to patiently endure me banging on about this story for the past couple of years. I have got it out of my system now but thank you all for putting up with me in the process.

There are also a number of people who have taken an interest in this book over the years and have offered valuable insights into its final shape. These include Steve Abbott, Alex Dickson, Olivia Fox, Susan Lowenstein, James Hamilton and Alison Webb. I am grateful to them all.

Finally, I would really like to make special mention of

the one man who made all of this possible. This is my eighth book and none of them would have happened had it not been for Richard Attenborough having had the decency and the humanity to cooperate with an unpublished author for my first book *The Actors' Director*. All of this stemmed from that and if I can never thank him sufficiently, I am unutterably happy to be able to acknowledge the debt.

*Andy Dougan*

1. Georgy Timofeyev.  4. Pavel Komarov.

2. Nikolai Trusevich.  5. Alexei Klimenko.

3. Ivan Kuzmenko.  6. Nikolai Korotkykh.

7. Vasily Sukharev.

8. Feodor Tyutchev.

9. Makar Goncharenko.

10. Mikhail Putistin.

11. Mikhail Melnik.

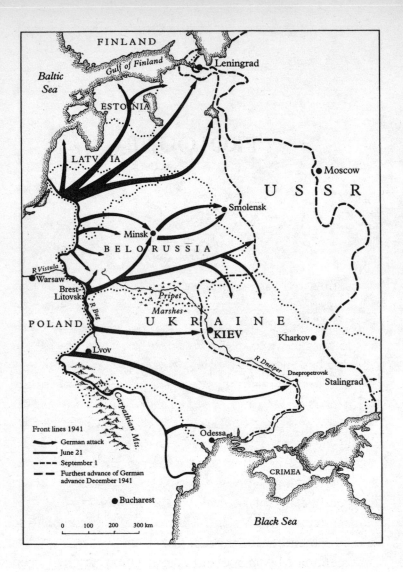

FINLAND

*Baltic Sea*

*Gulf of Finland*

Leningrad

ESTONIA

LATVIA

USSR

Moscow

Smolensk

Minsk

BELORUSSIA

R Vistula

Warsaw

Brest-Litovsk

Pripet Marshes

R Bug

POLAND

UKRAINE

KIEV

Kharkov

Lvov

R Dneiper

Dnepropetrovsk

Stalingrad

Carpathian Mts.

Front lines 1941

→ German attack

—— June 21

---- September 1

▬▬ Furthest advance of German
advance December 1941

Odessa

CRIMEA

● Bucharest

0   100   200   300 km

*Black Sea*

# PROLOGUE

## 21 JUNE 1941

Valentina and Alexei were very much in love, a blind man on a galloping horse could see that. It was the little things that gave them away, like the fact that they just could not take their eyes off each other. Valentina was in the kitchen with the other women while Alexei was outside smoking with the men. But no matter where they went or how far they strayed within the big apartment they always found each other with their eyes. Alexei could hear her laughing with her friends, it was an excited girlish laugh which was not at all fitting for her serious job as a laboratory worker. But no one would grudge her any of her enjoyment on this, her big day. This, after all, was Valentina's wedding day, the day she would remember for the rest of her life.

Valentina Masterova and Alexei Dubovsky had been married earlier that afternoon. It had been a traditional ceremony that had taken place on a glorious midsummer's day, so the omens were good for a long and happy marriage. They had not known each other long but they loved each other; that they had no place to stay and no real plans did not seem to matter. They had good jobs – he was an engineer and she worked in the laboratory – and they had each other. That was what was important. Why should it matter that they were starting their married life in someone else's house? Since they had no apartment of their own they were holding their wedding banquet at a flat which belonged to one of Valentina's girlfriends. The apartment was big and airy, the sort of place they would have loved for themselves, but despite its space it was crammed to the rafters with friends and well-wishers. There was one other added attraction to the apartment on the corner of Lenin Street, it was above the best bakery in Kiev, Bakery no. 3. Valentina worked in the laboratories checking the quality of the bread and the purity of the wheat while Alexei and his fellow engineers kept the place running. Almost everyone they knew worked at the bakery and it was at a works social function where they themselves had first met. But even a works celebration could not match what was on offer here today.

The groaning tables which filled the large living room were ample testament to the skill and craft of the workers at the bakery downstairs. This was a special occasion and everyone seemed to have made a special effort to make sure that their contribution was as rich, as soft, as perfect as it could be for the happy couple. There were breads of all shapes and sizes and description; good white wheat bread and rich black rye bread. With the bread there was smoked salmon and caviar, expensive to be sure but it was not every day a girl got married. The salmon and caviar were a treat, something to be savoured, but everyone else had pitched in with the rest of the meal. There were *vareniki* – dumplings stuffed with cottage cheese – and, to eat with them, bowls of *smetana* – sour cream – that could also be added to the plates of soup being ladled out of huge tureens by the enthusiastic guests. There was *borscht* of course, and *schi* – cabbage soup – and some pungent *rassolnik* – a kind of meat soup – as well as delicious *ukha* – fish soup. The room was filled with a heady mixture of aromas as the strong smells and flavours of traditional Ukrainian cooking vied with each other. Huge plates were piled high with mounds of pork and beef, other pots contained rich and intoxicating stews. Every time the piles looked like dwindling another guest would arrive with a pot or a plate of something delicious to add to the menu. One table contained nothing but fish dishes. Since they were on the banks of the Dnieper and not too far from the Black Sea the quality of seafood was superb. Apart from the salmon and caviar there was marinated herring as well as plates and plates of *vobla* – the sharp-tasting, salt-covered dried fish.

The guests helped themselves throughout the day, attacking the laden tables with increasing enthusiasm. The enthusiasm was fuelled by large amounts of alcohol. The local vodka called *gorilka* was consumed with gusto. The drink takes its name from the Ukrainian word for burning, but the rough nature of the liquor did not appear to be deterring anyone from drinking it. The women drank with as much delicacy as they could muster from the small glasses known as *ryumka*, while the hardier men slaked their thirst with gusto from the larger *stakan*, which held just over half a pint. Each swill of vodka was accompanied by a handful of olives or a tangy portion of savoury, fatty *salo* to soak up the alcohol. There were copious quantities of beer too and given the heat of the summer's day there were pitchers and pitchers of *kvas*. This cold concoction made from dark rye bread and yeast, kept cool in assorted pantries and cupboards, was like ambrosia on such a warm day.

As the day wore on the guests became more and more tipsy, but no one was really drunk, or badly behaved. They seemed to be as intoxicated by the balmy evening air wafting in through the long since thrown open windows as they were by anything they had drunk. There was scarcely a breeze that night and the open windows did little to reduce the temperature in the room. Pungent clouds of cigarette smoke rose towards the high ceiling where they gathered and hung for a time before drifting out into the night. As the room became warmer the guests became less inhibited. The men had shed their jackets and opened their shirts, while the women, emboldened by drink and good humour, laughed with and teased prospective consorts. The flowers woven in their hair were slowly coming undone, the brightly coloured ribbons they had threaded through their braids were unravelling. A slightly reckless, giddy mood took hold of the party. The young men told more and more exaggerated stories as they tried to impress the young women, the older folk simply sat and smiled and made the odd knowing remark to each other about the likely outcome of these courtships. Which young girl would lose more than a hair ribbon; which of the young bucks would emerge dominant; and whose heart would be broken next. It was a raucous gathering but good-

4

natured as everyone allowed the cares of the world to drift away. There would be sore heads in the morning and work again on Monday, but that was all too far away.

Out on the balcony Dubovsky stood and looked down on the street below. He could hear Valentina laughing with her friends and from the tone of her laugh it had doubtless been at some comment about the night ahead. Dubovsky was looking for late-comers, perhaps someone who might have lost their way or did not know the apartment. As he stood and smoked he waved occasionally to passers-by who called up their congratulations or to old women sitting on their own balconies further down Lenin Street as they watched the world go by. A formal guest list had been something of a notional concept, although he could not help but notice there were two notable absentees from the party. The first was Iosif Kordik, a taciturn little man who was a manager of another bakery nearby and who would inevitably have found something to complain about amidst all the festivities. He would not be missed and Dubovsky frankly would have been sorry to see him turn the corner and head up to the apartment. Kordik, who had been invited as a friend of a friend, had hinted that he might not be able to make the party because of family commitments. Dubovsky was mildly surprised because he was not even certain that Kordik had any family and suspected it was merely a polite excuse. Nonetheless he had not pressed the matter. Perhaps, it occurred to him now, he should have. Kordik was an important man and a man with some influence in the city. It would not do to offend him.

The other absentee was much more disappointing.

Dubovsky had considered it a bit of a coup when Konstantin Shchegotsky had accepted an invitation to the wedding. Shchegotsky was something of a catch. Dubovsky knew him through a mutual acquaintance and he was delighted when Kostya – he felt he knew him well enough to be so familiar – had replied saying he would come. Konstantin Shchegotsky was the darling of the young intelligentsia in Kiev, not that Dubovsky considered himself in that class but he had aspirations which could surely only be improved by having Kostya at his wedding reception. Not only famous as one of the country's best footballers, Shchegotsky was also notorious as a man of a dark and dangerous reputation. No woman was safe, so they said, as he flitted easily between Kiev and Moscow fitting in effortlessly into whatever circle he chose to include himself. Tall, athletic but at the same time vulnerably and attractively thin, Shchegotsky brought out the protective instincts in women of all ages. He had acquired a reputation as something of a ladies' man almost without trying. With his sharp clothes, his imported cigarettes, and his taste for high living he was the sort of man whose company men also sought. They never felt threatened by him, it was almost an honour to be included in his circle. A couple of years earlier he had dropped out of sight for over a year with no explanation. The rumours circulated that he had been having a passionate affair with the wife of a high-ranking Scandinavian diplomat and had been advised to lie low until the scandal blew over. It was a period that Shchegotsky never talked about, which only added to his air of mystique and his aura of wounded fragility. As the afternoon wore on into the evening

Dubovsky resigned himself to the inevitability that Kostya would not be coming. If truth be told he had never really believed that someone as important as Shchegotsky would have come to his wedding, but he had hoped. Dubovsky was disappointed, of course, but nowhere near as disappointed as the young single women at the party, as well as a few who were not so young and not so single.

While the revellers were becoming increasingly rowdy Konstantin Shchegotsky had sought and was enjoying his own company. He would have liked to have been at the wedding. He liked Alexei and Valentina, they were a good couple, and he was seldom one to miss out on a party. Other considerations took precedence that night, however, which was why he was out walking in the late summer evening along the Boulevard Shevchenko, the street named after the serf who had become the national poet of the Ukraine. Kostya was thinking about the day ahead. It held a big game for him and his friends and he wanted to be sure he was as ready for it as he could be. As he walked aimlessly he found himself back at his hotel. He stopped in the doorway to finish his cigarette and took in the beauty of the city for a few moments. Even at this late hour the air was thick with the heavy fragrance of the flowers which seemed to be everywhere. There was by now a slight breeze, barely enough to rustle the branches in the chestnut trees, and certainly not enough to cool down the heat of the day. Kostya took one last draw on his cigarette, flicked the butt into the gutter with his thumb and forefinger, and strolled slowly past the concierge and up to his room.

As Shchegotsky turned in for the night there was no

sign of the party slowing down over at Bakery no. 3. The beer and the wine and the *gorilka* still flowed like water, the songs and laughter could be heard floating halfway down the street. People left in twos and threes but there was still a hard core from the bakery drinking and revelling their way into the early hours. Finally, as dawn broke, they took their leave of the newly-weds and left them to what remained of their wedding night with risqué salutations and bawdy exhortations. Their parting was not peaceful and even as they left they shouted promises to each other to meet up again in the afternoon. A few hours' sleep and they would be fit enough to catch the festivities to mark the opening of the new sports stadium. It was five o'clock in the morning before the last party-goers made their drunken way to bed. A few of them insisted they could hear thunder. Others maintained it was the sound of blasting and wondered why they would be working on the new waterworks on a Sunday.

Over at his hotel Konstantin Shchegotsky was awakened by the phone ringing. He could tell from the half-light outside that it was very early. He picked up his watch from the bedside table and looked at it. It was barely six. Who would call at an hour like this on a day like this?

It was his friend Gurevich. 'Kostya, the war has started,' he said.

'Stop joking,' Shchegotsky replied. 'How much did you have to drink at the wedding?'

'No, Kostya,' Gurevich insisted. 'I'm not joking. Listen to me. It has begun. The Fascists have attacked us.'

The phone clicked off as Gurevich hung up. Shchegotsky looked at the receiver for a moment and began to wonder if he had imagined the conversation. He went to the window and opened the *fortochka* – the small window inset into the larger one – to look out. Everything was quiet. Down below he could see the night janitor out sweeping the doorstep and getting ready to hose down the pavement.

Shchegotsky was still trying to make sense of it all when he too heard the distant explosions.

# CHAPTER ONE

The Ukraine stretches from Belarus in the north to the natural border of the Black Sea in the south, but its western and eastern borders have always been open to negotiation. In the west, the rising Carpathians form a geological boundary with Poland, Slovakia and Hungary, but the political boundaries have not always been so clearly defined. Similarly in the east the border with the Russian Federation has concertinaed in and out over the centuries.

What has remained unchanged is the heart of the Ukraine, a vast expanse – 1,600 kilometres wide, roughly the size of France – of flat, rich farmland. The soil is as black as the Ukraine's other natural treasure the coal, which is found in such abundance in the Donbas region. The crops that grow in this fertile soil fed the rest of the country to the point where the Ukraine became known as the breadbasket of the Soviet Union. But the massive steppe which blessed the Ukraine with its rich harvests has also proved to be its greatest curse. Such vast bounty will always attract rapacious predators and the endless tracts of gently undulating land have proved almost impossible to defend against successive invaders.

Such was the case in the middle of the eleventh century when the Pechenegs, a nomadic race from the north, set their sights on the Ukraine. They had staged a number of harrying raids on the borders of what would later become the Ukrainian state but in 1036 they were about to strike directly at the heart of Kiev. As the Pechenegs made their camp just outside the city walls the Kievan king, Yaroslav the Wise, was distraught with a mixture of grief and rage at seeing his enemy so close to his city. Yaroslav sought succour in the Blessed Virgin. If she would help defeat his enemy then he would build a great church in her honour. The battle for Kiev was fierce and bloody but Yaroslav prevailed and the Pechenegs were routed. True to his promise he built the magnificent Cathedral of St Sophia on the spot where the battle was won and dedicated it to the honour of the Blessed Virgin. The cathedral presented Yaroslav with a new problem. Magnificent though it was, it now extended the city boundaries and would have to be defended. Yaroslav ordered that new ramparts and defences be built and in the midst of these new city walls he ordered a great gate to be built. The city could already be entered by the Liadsky Gate on the eastern side and the Lvivsky Gate on the western side, but neither of these could compare with this new monument.

The Great Golden Gate of Kiev was twelve metres high with an arch which was twenty-five metres long. From outer wall to outer wall it measured almost eight metres wide. The foundations were three metres deep and the walls were a metre thick. Onlookers were dazzled by the sunlight reflected from the huge granite and quartzite boulders that made up the arch. The effect was set off with doors which were made of oak but held together by sheets of gilded copper. On top of the tower above the gate was a small chapel, the Church of the Annunciation of the Blessed Virgin Mary, because Yaroslav was still a devout and grateful man.

It was an architectural miracle. Although not written until 1874, the soaring triumphalism of the first few notes of 'The Great Gate of Kiev', from Ukrainian composer Modest Mussorgsky's *Pictures at an Exhibition*, give some idea of the awe and wonder which this incomparable structure must have invoked.

But even when the Great Golden Gate was built in the eleventh century the city was already old and battle-scarred. The history of Kiev has been shot through with periods of violent conflict and lengthy occupation since it was founded, probably sometime around the fourth century AD. The city sits on the hills overlooking the River Dnieper. The Dnieper is one of the great water-ways of Europe. At 2,200 kilometres long it is the fourth longest river on the continent. From its source in the Valdai Hills just west of Moscow it runs south through Belarus, and the very heart of the Ukraine, including Kiev and Dnipropetrovsk, before emptying into the Black Sea. Kiev itself was established on the right, or western, bank of the river before expanding through the centuries to the left bank as well. It is often referred to as 'The Mother of Russian Cities' and with good cause.

During the second half of the ninth century a band of Vikings known as Varangians were marauding southwards looking for fresh lands to settle. In 862 the

Varangian leader Rurik became ruler of the Russian city of Novgorod and established Varangians as a presence in the region. Twenty years later another Varangian, called Oleg, who was acting as regent for Rurik's young son Igor, saw the strategic importance of Kiev and its ability to control the river. He had the rulers of the city executed and united Kiev with Novgorod. Oleg settled in Kiev which thus became, in 882, the capital of the first Russian state, which was known as the Kievan Rus. The beginnings of what became known as the Russian Empire were therefore set in the ninth century in a confederacy of states which was ruled from Kiev.

The importance of the city of Kiev cannot be over-estimated. Its position on the Dnieper made it a vital trading centre and the river itself became a major trade route. Over the next century the size and influence of the Kievan Rus increased. In 988 Vladimir the Great, some-times also called St Vladimir, embraced Byzantine Christianity, making Kiev the original centre of Christianity in Russia. Because of the flat geography which offered little hindrance to any would-be marauder and its exposed position close to the Russian frontier, Kiev became a target for almost every invading army over sub-sequent years. Yaroslav may have been able to drive off the Pechenegs in 1036 but the city was all but destroyed by the Mongol leader Batu Khan in 1240 and remained in the hands of the Mongolian hordes for the next century.

It was during the time of the Mongol occupation when perhaps the region's greatest hero rose to prominence. In the same year that Kiev was invaded by Batu Khan, Alexander, the son of Yaroslav the prince of the state of Vladimir, won a great and stirring battle against the

Swedes on the ice-covered River Neva near St Petersburg. He took the name Alexander Nevsky in honour of his famous victory. Two years later Alexander, who was a prince of Novgorod, drove off the Teutonic Knights in another famous battle at Lake Peipus in Estonia. This battle was later credited with saving Russia from domination by the West. Batu Khan the Mongol leader recognised Alexander's influence and rather than fight him he enlisted Alexander as a mediator between his Golden Horde and the people of the Kievan Rus. In 1246 Alexander was made Grand Prince of Kiev by the Mongols and six years later he was also made prince of Vladimir. With the three great cities of Kiev, Novgorod and Vladimir under his control, Alexander was able to stabilise and solidify the region and did much to ensure the beginnings of what we now know as the Russian Federation. Alexander died in 1263 and was later canonised by the Russian Orthodox church.

Almost a century later, the city changed hands again. The Lithuanians seized it in 1360, then in 1482 it fell to Tartars from the Crimea before it was ultimately taken by Poland in 1569.

The seventeenth century saw the advent of another great Ukrainian hero when Bohdan Khmelnytsky led a Cossack uprising against the Poles in 1648. The Cossacks were superb horsemen and inspired by their leaders, known as hetmans, they used the huge expanse of the steppe to their advantage as they harried and pursued the Poles in a series of cavalry battles. Khmelnytsky and the hetmans were able to successfully establish an independent Ukrainian republic, but their autonomy was short-lived. The region was still a target for the various conflicting neighbours that surrounded it and in 1654, just six years after winning independence, Khmelnytsky had to ask for Russian protection. This then led to a bitter war between Russia, Poland, the Cossacks and Turkey for control of the Ukraine. The war was ended by the so-called 'Eternal Peace' between Russia and Poland in 1686 in which Kiev and the Cossack lands east of the Dnieper were handed over to Russia. This was really a recognition of the status quo by the Poles who, since they could not defeat the Cossacks, had decided simply to leave them with Russia to which they had allied themselves in the first place. The rest of the Ukraine was given to Poland, but after a second partition of Poland in 1793 the whole of present-day Ukraine – with the exception of the province of Galicia which remained under Austro-Hungarian rule – came under the influence of Russia.

During the Russian Revolution of 1917 another attempt was made to set up an independent Ukrainian state that was even more short-lived than Khmelnytsky's efforts. The Red Army occupied Kiev in January 1918 but in March of the same year the Germans took over the city under the Treaty of Brest-Litovsk which was designed to end hostilities in the region. The Germans were looking forward to a new supply of rich, fertile land and the new nationalist government of Simon Petlyura was looking forward to independence from their Bolshevik neighbours. Nothing went as either side had planned. The Petlyura government was woefully in-effective and only a few weeks after the assembly had been set up the Germans disbanded it in what amounted to an armed coup. Finally with the war in France going against them the Germans abandoned Kiev and the Ukraine. Petlyura came back and so too did the Red Army. The eighteen months that followed are probably the most volatile in the history of any modern country. Some sources say Kiev changed hands or changed governments as often as eighteen times in that period. The final outcome was that by 1922 Kiev and the Ukraine were formally incorporated as one of the Union of Soviet Socialist Republics (USSR).

They were now in the USSR but the Ukrainians do not appear to have been of the USSR. Perversely, the successive changes of government and controlling nations helped to promote an increased feeling of Ukrainian nationalism. It did not matter who was in charge, at the end of the day they were still Ukrainians and their allegiance to their country, to each other, and to the ground they stood on was all that mattered.

Although the country was technically at peace, the arguments between Ukrainian nationalism and Bolshevism continued unabated for almost twenty years. The Ukrainians had good reason to distrust Lenin. After the Russian Revolution and a brief period of Ukrainian independence, he had gone back on his word and sent in the Red Army. The result was that by 1920 the Ukraine was, in name at least, largely Bolshevik. Lenin, and after him Stalin, remained convinced that the Ukrainians' urge for nationalism had only been suppressed and not extinguished. To some extent they were correct and both men harboured a deep distrust of the Ukraine. That distrust would account for the terrible suffering that awaited the Ukraine in the years before the Second World War.

By the end of the twenties famine caused by desperate shortages of meat and grain stalked the new Soviet Union. In 1921 and 1922 five million people died through starvation and the associated diseases of typhus, cholera and dysentery. People were living on a ration of 200 grams of bread per day and regarded with a mixture of incredulity and envy reports that in Petrograd some skilled workers were being allocated as much as 800 grams a day. People fled the cities into the country in search of food. The population of Moscow, for example, dropped by almost half in the three years after the Revolution. The rural communities had both meat and grain, but because what they produced was being requisitioned, their response was simply to produce less. There was no incentive to produce anything more than what they needed for themselves. The official price of grain, for example, was less than it cost to grow and even if farmers were inclined to barter there was nothing in the cities they wanted. Instead they simply stored it or ate it. The rural communities were a constant thorn in the flesh to Stalin and Lenin before him. Unlike in the cities which were areas of dense population, communism did not have much of an impact on the agrarian population which at that time still made up some 80 per cent of the Soviet Union. Stalin's solution to the shortages in the cities and the relative plenty in the country was to bring in a policy of collectivisation with every head of cattle, every ear of grain, every bushel of wheat becoming the property of the state. Anyone attempting to profit for themselves would be severely punished. Under the so-called 'Seven Eighths Law' – it was passed on 7 August 1932, the seventh day of the eighth month – anyone who cut even a single ear of corn could be, and frequently was, sentenced to ten years in a labour camp. Stalin's policy exploited the jealousy and greed born of real suffering and, in the very antithesis of communist philosophy, turned neighbour against neighbour.

Stalin declared war on the 'kulaks'. This was a new classification which the officials had devised when they came to categorise the peasants. They could be split into three classes – poor, middle, and kulak, a word that although it meant 'fist' had passed into common usage as a derogatory term for a moneylender. Basically, a kulak was a farmer who had shown enough enterprise to build his farm into a size where it was necessary to hire help to work it. But on 30 January 1930 Stalin announced that all farms were to be collectivised and the kulaks were to be destroyed as a class. There were three penalties for being a kulak. The most severe offenders were shot, and their families joined those in the second category who faced deportation to labour camps, while the third category were forced to leave the collective and start up again on a new farm. As one final sadistic twist, these new farms were without exception sited on land which could not be cultivated, otherwise it would have been part of the collective to begin with. After months of back-breaking toil these unfortunates were unable to meet their quota to the collective and were deported anyway.

The process of 'dekulakisation' produced an orgy of pettiness and betrayal as neighbours settled scores by accusing others of being kulaks. Once the accusation had been made there was almost no way of disproving it and, even if the accused was fortunate enough to disprove the case, they were invariably tagged as kulak sympathisers and therefore still liable to be punished. Between 1930 and 1933 some 2 million people were sent to Corrective Labour Camps in remote areas such as Siberia. Few of them returned. The Ukraine which was the breadbasket of the Soviet Union was particularly hard hit by the war against the kulaks and the collectivisation which followed.

Stalin continued to doubt that the Ukraine, in particular, was wholehearted or enthusiastic in its endorsement of communism. He believed that the Ukraine would much rather be a separate state and was wary of these nationalist tendencies. One way of dealing with this was to ensure that the region was treated far more harshly than anywhere else. At one point more than 70 per cent of Ukrainian peasants were working on collective farms, a much higher figure than anywhere else in the Soviet Union. The effect of the collectivisation was to force down what had been an abundant harvest. In 1931 the official harvest was down to 18 million tons, a figure which represented just enough to feed everyone with a little surplus left over. Nonetheless the state demanded almost 8 million tons of this harvest, leaving the Ukraine on the point of starvation. The consequences were inevitable. The following year the harvest dropped to just over 14 million tons and once again the state demanded almost 8 million. This was later reduced to a little over 6.5 million tons but the effect was the same. Starvation was rife and millions of Ukrainians perished in what came to be known as the Great Hunger. Those who survived knew that this famine had been artificially engineered solely as a result of Stalin's policies. Official figures for the death toll in the Ukraine are not known but the generally accepted estimates place the number of dead in 1932–3 at somewhere between 5 million and 7 million. In the Soviet Union as a whole the number of deaths in this politically-induced famine is put at 14 million, but as Khrushchev later famously remarked 'no one was keeping count'. Indeed the official census of 1937 showed that the population had dropped so alarmingly that those organising the census were among the victims of Stalin's purges for 'treasonably exerting themselves to diminish the population of the USSR'.

Apart from those who had starved in the Great Hunger there were also a great many people in Kiev who had suffered at the hands of the NKVD in the thirties during what became known as 'the Terror'. The NKVD were the successors of OGPU, the organisation which had handled the deportation of the kulaks to the wastes of Siberia. Only the name had changed, in essence they were still Stalin's secret police, enforcers of his singular will by any means necessary. It was the NKVD who were behind the dreaded knock on the door in the night that usually resulted in interrogation, torture, a show trial and then death or deportation, although in many cases these were effectively the same thing. Thousands of good and experienced Red Army officers had fallen victim to these trials on trumped up accusations of disloyalty or being bourgeois.

Again, Stalin's pathological distrust of the Ukraine was manifest in the Terror. In 1937 he had decided to liquidate the entire leadership of the Ukrainian Soviet and the local Communist Party. By the following June the seventeen most senior ministers had been arrested and executed and the Prime Minister of the Ukrainian

Soviet, Liubchenko, had killed himself. It is estimated that around 170,000 people in the Ukraine were expunged, prompting Nikita Khrushchev, who was now in Kiev as the First Secretary of the Communist Party, to remark that the Ukrainian Party had been purged spotless.

In the Ukraine, as everywhere else in the USSR, the victims of the Terror had nothing in common except their misfortune. One unfortunate industrialist was jailed for ten years because he had been the first to sit down during a standing ovation for Comrade Stalin. Another newspaper editor was purged because he was Jewish. A man reportedly fell victim for removing a portrait of Stalin while he was painting the wall behind it.

In Kiev alone one woman is alleged to have denounced 8,000 people, all of whom were put to death. The Terror thrived on denunciation. Worker informed on workmate, brother on brother, husband on wife. They may have begun believing they were doing the right thing, but by 1938 when the Terror was at its height people were denouncing others simply out of fear of being denounced themselves, thus getting their revenge in first. The greatest crime was the catch-all accusation of being 'bourgeois'. The charge was practically impossible to disprove: almost anything could be interpreted as evidence of bourgeois behaviour.

There were some, like Konstantin Shchegotsky, who were high profile targets. Despite being a good and loyal Stalinist, Shchegotsky's lifestyle antagonised a great many within the Party. He was handsome, popular, well-liked, a social gadfly, something of a womaniser, and a hero to the bright young things of Moscow and Kiev.

Shchegotsky inspired jealousy almost effortlessly and given the flamboyance of his lifestyle it is perhaps not surprising that he attracted attention.

Even though his lifestyle was a little wayward and extravagant, occasionally bordering on the indiscreet, Shchegotsky was respected by the Communist Party for his skills as a footballer and a sportsman. In 1938 he was given a decoration by the Party for his services to sport and, as was the custom, the award was announced in the newspapers. At the time he was in a sanatorium recovering from a football injury. His room-mate there wrote to the Party organisation complaining that obviously Shchegotsky did not value his decoration sufficiently to wear it. Shchegotsky was summoned to answer the accusations and when the local Party secretary told him of the charges he simply laughed. Shchegotsky pointed out that the story in the newspaper had merely been the announcement of his decoration, he had not yet received the medal. His accuser was brought to confront him, but Shchegotsky laughed in his face.

'I do not wear it because I have not been given it,' said Shchegotsky. 'Once I receive it I shall wear it proudly.'

Shchegotsky was allowed to leave without a blemish on his reputation – although he would not be so fortunate on another occasion – and his accuser then had to answer charges himself for having denounced such a faithful servant of the Soviet Union.

# CHAPTER TWO

Football seems to have arrived in the Ukraine in much the same way that it was introduced to the rest of the world: it came from Britain. The game of football spread from its British origins at the end of the nineteenth and beginning of the twentieth century as a direct consequence of Britain's seafaring dominance. The South American countries, for example, whose players would dominate the game in the latter half of the twentieth century, learned to play football originally from Scottish and English sailors who called in at Montevideo, Rio de Janeiro, Caracas and other major ports on the trade routes. In the Ukraine, there are two schools of thought on the matter. One claims that the game was introduced by Czech engineers who were working on local industrial projects, but this seems to be a revisionist theory designed to deprive the imperialists of any credit for a sport which began as an eccentric hobby and turned into one of the Soviet Union's national pastimes. The more credible theory is that football came to the Ukraine as a consequence of locals being intrigued by, and then attempting to emulate, the British sailors who would amuse themselves by having kick-abouts when their ships were laid over in Odessa.

It is certain that British sailors played football in the Ukraine towards the end of the 1870s, probably around 1878, and within a very few years it had captured the imagination of the whole region. The game started in the western Ukraine but quickly spread. Professor Cenar, apparently an instant enthusiast for the new sport, published in 1891 a monograph entitled *Sporting Games of School Youth*. This talked about football development programmes being followed in various local schools. Apart from being one of the earliest Soviet sports writers, Professor Cenar is also responsible for perhaps the most significant development in the history of the local game. In 1890 the professor arranged through various academic contacts to have the first genuine football brought to Lviv from Britain. As well as providing a real ball, quickly copied by local manufacturers, Professor Cenar was responsible for football officially becoming part of Ukrainian culture.

The town of Lviv is only fifty miles away from the border between the Ukraine and Poland and from 1773 until the collapse of the Austro-Hungarian Empire in 1918 it was ruled by Austria. In 1892 the emperor Franz-Joseph had the idea of holding biennial fairs which would highlight local trade and culture. By 1892, sport had become an integral part of the local culture and was therefore entitled to a place in the fair. However Professor Cenar, the secretary of the organising committee, and a local sports reporter who was the chairman used their powers of persuasion to convince their fellow members that football should also be included. The other rapidly growing sport of cycling was also given official recognition in that 1892 fair. The first official football demonstration in Lviv took place on 5 June 1892. This was not by any means a competitive game, it was simply a demonstration of heading and ball-juggling skills that entertained the crowd during a break in a gymnastics competition. The football demonstration turned out to be a huge success, so much so that by May 1894 when the second fair was held a new stadium had been built in Stryisky Park. The ground had a capacity of 7,000 and in keeping with everything else connected with Ukrainian football up to that time, it was modelled on the British style with grandstands and terraces.

The new stadium was inaugurated with the first official competitive football match to be played in the Ukraine. The game, on 14 July 1894, between the cities of Lviv and Kraków was held as part of the second congress of Sokil, the society of Ukrainian sport. No mere demonstration of skills, this was the first official match on Ukrainian soil involving local players and it was played under the current rules of Association Football. The match was such an event that the stadium was filled to more than its capacity – no one has been able to accurately estimate the crowd – and it attracted reporters from Czechoslovakia, Germany and Belarus as well as the Ukraine and Poland. The first written match report appeared three days later on the back page of the local newspaper *Hazeta Lvivska*. The game is also mentioned in *Himnastychny Putivnyk* in an article by Xavier Fischer who covered the second Sokil congress.

Thanks to Fischer we know that both teams wore white shirts and sports shoes rather than football boots. They were only distinguished by their trousers. Lviv wore grey sports pants and Kraków wore blue. The referee was a Professor Wyrobek from Kraków and the game lasted less than ten minutes. The teams had agreed beforehand that the first goal would settle the game and it duly did with Lviv scoring in the seventh minute to take the match. That game, brief though it was, was a touchstone for the development of football in the Ukraine. One of the suggested reasons for the world-wide success of football is that, apart from the game's intrinsic qualities, it is a remarkably simple game which almost anyone can play. This seems to have been a major influence in the spread of the sport in the Ukraine. There was no need to train arduously, and often repetitively, for hours on specialist apparatus as the gymnasts did, and, unlike the cyclists, you did not require a bicycle or a cycling track. All that was needed was a ball, some space and the participation of enthusiastic comrades. Football took off. By 1914 the first international club match had been played in the Ukraine. The Turkish side Fenerbahce came to Odessa on a goodwill tour from the other side of the Black Sea. They lost 2–1 to Sheremetievtsi, they then drew 1–1 with Sporting before United of Odessa beat them 3–0 and finally in two games against Sport Club of Mykolaiv they won 1–0 and lost 3–0. Having won one, drawn one, and lost three it was hardly the most successful tour Fenerbahce would ever undertake, but the goodwill generated was enormous. Each game was played in front of a capacity crowd with thousands more locked out and straining to judge how the game was going from the roars of those inside the ground.

Football had gone very quickly from being an amusing

diversion to a fanatical pastime for hundreds of thousands of young Ukrainians. Teams sprang up almost everywhere and soon the demand meant that competitions and leagues had to be established. Most of the teams came from existing sports clubs within factories, schools, offices and military units. Nikolai Khanikov and Sergei Barminsky were two young policemen who were members of Dynamo, the sports club of the police and the Ministry of Interior in Kiev. There were branches of this sports club in most major cities of the Soviet Union, the most notable was probably Dynamo Moscow whose football team was a major force in the Moscow championship. In November 1927 Khanikov and Barminsky set up Dynamo Kiev, then a team entirely composed of local police officers. There is some confusion over their first official match. The official club history says that it took place in July 1928 in Moscow, inevitably against Dynamo Moscow, and that Kiev lost 6–2. There are, however, reports that Kiev played their first game against a local team from Belaya Tserkov, a nearby town, and lost 2–1. Another account has Dynamo Kiev playing for the first time at their own Red Stadium on 17 July 1928 when they fought out a 2–2 draw with Odessa. Regardless of whichever match is named as their first official game it is fairly obvious that Dynamo Kiev were not immediately a great side. In 1929 the first international match in Dynamo Kiev's history took place on 14 September when Kiev lost 4–3 to Lower Austria.

Although in later years Dynamo would become the pre-eminent team in the Ukraine and the Soviet Union and a major force in world football, at its outset it was not even the best team in Kiev. Their local rivals Zheldor – also known as Lokomotiv – were the most powerful team in the area in the late twenties. Like Dynamo, Zheldor were effectively a works team. As the Lokomotiv name suggests, the side was made up largely of workers from the South Western Railway System. But the real power base in Ukrainian football at that period was Kharkov which had several strong teams.

In the absence of any formal national championships, teams from the various Soviet Republics competed on a regional basis. The Ukraine was generally represented in those matches by one of the sides from Kharkov, which was still the capital of the Ukrainian Soviet Socialist Republic. However the fortunes of Dynamo Kiev were about to improve dramatically.

As the competitiveness of the leagues intensified professionalism started to creep into the game. It became obvious that including only railwaymen or policemen in the team was a selection policy that would invite frequent defeat. It was not long before the game began to be dominated by players who were effectively professionals. These talented players, spotted playing for other local teams, would then be offered terms by one of the bigger clubs, which invariably meant a job in the relevant sector. For these players it was an ideal arrangement. They were given jobs which usually paid a little above the going rate yet the job itself generally allowed a lot of time off for football training. If they won their game they were paid a bonus, but even if they did not win they still had their week's wages from whatever organisation employed them. Under this sort of arrangement Russian footballers were never going to enjoy the lavish lifestyles of their modern counterparts, but they were able to live more comfortably than their fellow countrymen. In common with every other team in the country Dynamo Kiev were signing up professionals in the early 1930s, but they were extraordinarily fortunate in discovering a crop of young men who would go on to be some of the best players in the country.

One of the most outstanding talents, who was signed in 1930, was Nikolai Makhinya, a young man who had originally been something of a disappointment to his sports-mad family. He was born and raised in Podol, the oldest part of Kiev, and he and his two brothers and his sister all played sports. Nikolai however seemed to lag behind the others a little and when he was fourteen he was diagnosed as having a heart defect. Putting aside sports such as gymnastics and cycling Nikolai took up football instead. He surprised everyone by showing a tremendous natural ability. He played as an inside forward and despite his alleged heart condition he showed no signs of weakness or lack of stamina. Makhinya was a model player, a coach's dream. He did not smoke and he did not drink, he followed to the letter the training regime laid down by his coaches, and he spent very little time socialising after games. Makhinya was a serious-minded young man who lived only for his sport and his studies. He completed an apprenticeship as a metal turner before signing on as a student at the Institute of Physical Studies. Eventually his performances for local teams brought him to the attention of Dynamo Kiev. Evidently they had also heard about his medical history for Makhinya was required to endure a much more stringent physical examination than was usual for the time. To everyone's surprise, including possibly Makhinya's, the medical team who carried out the cardiac examination reported that 'with such a motor inside you, you could run until you are old'.

Along with Makhinya, Kiev had also signed Konstantin Shchegotsky, the intellectual and bon viveur. Despite a somewhat dilettante attitude, he was an equally devastating inside forward who became something of a glamorous media darling in his day. Both men had come from similar backgrounds. Makhinya had grown up as the son of a war veteran in straitened circumstances and become an almost slavish servant to the Party and Comrade Stalin. Shchegotsky, on the other hand, had chosen a life less dedicated to collectivisation and social responsibility, even though his impoverished upbringing was sadly typical of that of a great many children in post-Revolutionary Russia.

He was born in Moscow as the youngest of four children. Like so many others, the family circumstances were far from ideal and they were further complicated when his father died when he was barely a toddler. Konstantin was a thin and sickly child who was frequently looked after by neighbours while his mother and his siblings went out to work. Immediately after the Revolution, organised football in Moscow had been overwhelmed by political turmoil but the children still played. Konstantin was drafted into neighbourhood games and, because he was by far the smallest, the older boys kept an eye on him. They would play for hours in the garden of a nearby church and the games kept them out of trouble at a time when thousands of their contemporaries were ending up as beggars or criminals.

The constant exercise and the fresh air also helped Konstantin and before long he too became healthy and strong. Once their games outgrew the church garden, they moved to another makeshift pitch in a coal depot on the banks of the Moskva. The coal dust meant that every game finished with the players black as pitch and the normal post-match ritual, whatever the weather, involved a dip in the river to wash it off. Kostya was a poor swimmer and the after-match bath terrified him; on one occasion he almost drowned. Later in a memoir he recalled how he mastered his fear and within a year was able to swim back and forth across the river several times. This same dogged determination he had shown as a child would save his life as an adult.

With his full health and fitness Konstantin Shchegotsky was also precociously talented. He very quickly became captain of his street team and at the age of sixteen he was playing for Gornyak, a local senior side. Shchegotsky's role model at this stage was Pyotr Isakov who was one of the Soviet Union's footballing heroes. Isakov's trademark move involved trapping the ball on the touchline, luring the defender towards him, then turning through 180 degrees with the ball at his feet before racing away to leave the defender floundering in his wake. Kostya practised this move for hours and hours and even refined it to the point where he would do it in the middle of the pitch or in the penalty box, much to the frustration of opposing defenders or goalkeepers. It became a feature of his play. Shchegotsky was not a physically strong player in an age when physical strength was deemed the mark of a good player, but he was agile and quick and could deliver a pass with pinpoint accuracy. His debut for Gornyak was something of a local sensation. He scored a hat-trick in that first game and by the end of the match the word had gone out to local scouts that this young man was something special. Gornyak did better than expected in the Moscow championship, thanks largely to Shchegotsky, and when the team went bust in 1929 it was obvious that he was destined for greater things. Ironically his childhood illness, which we might reasonably guess to be rheumatic fever or something similar, meant that he had never officially been passed fit to take part in any kind of formal sporting activity. Perhaps it was this coupled with his slight build – his nickname was Schipa which translates as 'wood shaving' – that made some of the big clubs reluctant to give him the chance that his talent deserved. He could score goals and get round defenders but, as far as they were concerned, he could not tackle or barge anyone off the ball. Muscovite coaches wanted to see someone much stronger and the offers simply did not materialise. Although by his late teens Shchegotsky had qualified as a draughtsman and could have walked into a professional job, football had become his passion. He desperately wanted to find a team but no one in Moscow would have him. Then, just as he had all but given up hope of life as a footballer, he was offered terms by Dynamo Kiev in 1931 and was delighted to accept.

Both Shchegotsky and Makhinya were instant successes at Kiev, which had begun to grow in strength. The city itself was also regaining some of its old eminence and in 1934 it supplanted Kharkov as the capital of the Ukrainian Soviet Socialist Republic. Just as the capital shifted so too did the footballing power base.

In the 1932 Ukrainian championship Dynamo Kiev beat Kharkov 3–1 to take the title. This was a surprising result since Kharkov were generally regarded as the best club in the Ukraine. As a consequence of the victory Dynamo Kiev became the fashionable club, able to attract the best players. The upturn in the club's fortunes can be seen in the fact that on 20 August 1934 – less than seven years after it had been founded – Dynamo Kiev provided five players in the Ukrainian national side that beat Turkey 4–3. As well as Anton Idzkovsky in goal, Fyodor Tyutchev and Victor Shylovsky played in defence, and Shchegotsky and Makhinya formed part of the attack.

Further new talent continued to arrive, including perhaps the man who would be the most influential player at the club in the next decade. Nikolai Trusevich had started playing football when he was thirteen. Unlike Shchegotsky who began playing football when he was very young, Trusevich came to the game much older because of his family circumstances. Nikolai – Kolya to his friends – was born in Odessa in 1908 as one of a large family. His father found it difficult to find work and so Nikolai left school when he was only nine to do whatever he could to feed his brothers and sisters. There was no time for football or other sports, providing for his family was his overriding concern. As it happened he quite literally put bread on the table because he was quickly apprenticed at a local bakery and eventually became a master baker. It was his friends at the bakery who got him interested in football. Nikolai was tall and supple and they felt he had the makings of a perfect goalkeeper. But although he showed promise, the pressures of holding down a job, the anti-social hours at the bakery, providing for the rest of the family, and completing his studies in his spare time meant that football was something of a low priority for Trusevich. Even so he loved the game and played whenever he could. Eventually he was chosen regularly to play for an Odessan team called Pischevik, which was drawn from local food industry workers. Trusevich's talent was such that he very quickly moved to a larger team, signing for Dynamo Odessa in 1929. He played for Odessa for seven seasons and his unconventional style made him a huge favourite. He was a natural joker and there was a joyful exuberance about him. Odessa drew huge crowds every time they played and one of the main reasons was Trusevich and his eccentricities.

During the first half of the 1930s, the Dynamo Kiev goalkeeper was Anton Idzkovsky who was very famous in his own right. He and Nikolai became very close and he described the style which made Trusevich famous.

His style was very unusual. In those days the goalkeeper was considered quite classy if he could take the ball with his hands, like a cat. It was stylish to make very smooth dives to catch a low ball or very elegant leaps for a high ball. But Kolya had an entirely different manner. He would run quite far out of the goal and instead of catching the ball he would kick it. The crowd thought this was very unusual, a lot of them even thought it was funny, but Trusevich never seemed to mind.

As a goalkeeper Trusevich was well ahead of his time. At a time when the goalkeeper was seen simply as a last-ditch defender who seldom strayed from his goal line, Trusevich added an extra dimension to his game and gave his team more attacking options. His willingness to race off his line into his goal area meant that at times he was effectively an extra full-back. Although he enjoyed his time with Odessa, they were not a big club and whatever success they had derived from the solidity which Trusevich's skills gave them at the back. Everyone who watched him, Idzkovsky included, realised he was too big for the club. They urged him to move on and the obvious destination was Kiev. Trusevich signed for Dynamo in 1935.

Another skilful defender, Alexei Klimenko, joined at the same time. Klimenko was something of a local celebrity when he arrived in Kiev, because he was the youngest of three brothers who were part of a well-known circus family. His footballing career began in the unlikely location of Donbas, a coal-mining region in the south-east of the Ukraine. The Klimenkos were on tour and one of his brothers convinced the local Stakhanovits team to give young Alexei a trial after boasting of his footballing skills. A modest young man, Alexei none-theless impressed them with his talents and became a regular in their side. Before long his performances were good enough to attract his home town team. Alexei Klimenko was invariably known by the diminutive 'Sasha' because of his age, he was barely twenty, and his fresh-faced appearance. He was, however, a skilled and committed defender who would provide the club with the bedrock for some of its greatest victories.

By 1935 Dynamo Kiev were about to embark on a period which would see them emerge as one of the world's great footballing clubs. They were by now conspicuously the best team in the Ukraine, with their success firmly based on the talent at their disposal and not simply on an accident of geography. Their dominance in the Ukraine was firmly established in the summer of that year when, in a gesture of international solidarity, workers' groups in Belgium and France invited a national team from the Ukraine to come on tour and play a selection of local teams. The Ukrainian side contained no fewer than seven members of the Dynamo Kiev team and an eighth was soon to join them.

Anton Idzkovsky was first choice goalkeeper for both Dynamo Kiev and the Ukrainian national team, but after being selected he became ill and could not tour. His friend and understudy at Kiev, Nikolai Trusevich, was asked to take his place. The biggest game on the tour was an invitation match against Red Star Olympic, another communist team, in Paris. This was a major event for Dynamo since Red Star were a professional side and this was the first time in the history of Soviet football that its 'amateurs' would play against full-time footballers. Pre-match press comments do not appear to have changed in the sixty-odd years since that match took place. The French officials and manager indulged in the sort of psychological brinkmanship which is now commonplace before a European tie. The local French party officials assured the Ukrainians that their workers would give of their best, but Kiev were a great side and the French would consider themselves fortunate with a draw. The Red Star manager, however, was a little more forthright, saying that his players would go easy on the Ukrainians and try not to score too many goals.

There is no doubt that the big occasion did seem to affect the visiting players at first. When they went out on to the pitch before the game they were surprised by two things, the size of the crowd, and the fact that there was a fence separating the crowd from the players. Afterwards Trusevich recalled that as he scanned the Red Star line-up before the kick-off he could not help but notice that many of them looked at the Ukrainian players with complete contempt. However, he was not given much chance to dwell on the fact once the game was underway. The Kiev team seemed paralysed by the scale of the event and Red Star could and did attack at will. Trusevich's goal was under constant bombardment for the first twenty minutes of the game. The goalkeeper threw himself all over his goal, he leaped, he kicked, he dived at the feet of opposing forwards, and throughout it all he kept his goal intact. Slowly, the other Ukrainians began to take a greater part in the game. Inspired by Trusevich's heroics, they composed themselves and started to move the ball around. Once they had become accustomed to the stadium and the Red Star tactics, they grew in confidence and began to attack. The French were stunned when Nikolai Makhinya opened the scoring with a header. As they were starting to get over the loss of that goal, Makhinya struck again, this time with a volley, and the French found themselves further behind. By this stage Ukraine were flying. Shchegotsky was displaying his trademark pivot, leaving the French defence in tatters, and before half-time he managed to score, as did Victor Shylovsky.

At half-time the Red Star players, who had said they would not be too hard on the visitors, were 4–0 down.

There was also no sign of them having kept to their ironic promise to go easy. They had thrown everything they had at the Ukraine, but Trusevich had been superb in goal and his performance had inspired his team-mates. In the second half it was the Ukrainians who took things easily and turned the game into an exhibition match. Shylovsky was easily the most influential outfield player and he scored two more goals for his hat-trick. Trusevich was equally impressive in goal, but he was not unbeatable. Red Star, by all accounts a good side in their own right, did manage to get one past him and in the end the Ukraine won 6–1.

Having disposed of some of the best France had to offer, the rest of the tour was little more than a formality for the Ukrainians. They played a succession of trade union teams from France and Belgium and beat them all at a canter. By the time they returned home to the Ukraine they had scored eighty-eight goals and conceded only three. The importance of the Kiev players in the victorious campaign can be judged by the fact that three of them – Shchegotsky, Shylovsky and Fomin – were immediately drafted into the USSR national side.

Football was now well and truly established as a national sport in the Soviet Union and the first national club championship was played in 1936. There were two championships that year, one in the summer and another in the late autumn. Seven teams took part, each representing one of the Soviet Republics, and there was no doubt that Dynamo Kiev would represent the Ukraine. Dynamo began that first league campaign as one of the teams who were mentioned as potential winners. Their first game was at home on 24 May 1936 against Spartak of Moscow, who were the pre-championship favourites. Everyone expected a tough game but, to everyone's surprise, Kiev were comprehensively beaten 5–1 at home. Their only goal, their first of the championship, was scored by Nikolai Makhinya. The players and the fans were stunned but Kiev, who were perhaps guilty of believing the pre-tournament publicity, were able to put the defeat behind them and apply themselves more diligently. They concentrated on playing football rather than showing off, they worked on passing the ball fluidly and creatively and, as a consequence, won their next four games comfortably, taking them to second place in the league. So by the end of the season, Dynamo of Kiev were to face their old rivals Dynamo of Moscow, the team which had humbled them in one of their first competitive fixtures almost a decade earlier. This time there was the added incentive of winner takes all. Whoever won the game would be the first champions of the USSR.

A photograph taken before the start of that game has become one of the most famous in the club's history. It shows the Kiev team in their pale blue shirts and white shorts, lining up before the game in Moscow. Judging by what can be seen of the background, there is a huge crowd in the stadium. The players stand shoulder to shoulder on the halfway line with the look of men who know they can trust themselves and their team-mates to do what is required of them. The slender figure of Konstantin Shchegotsky looking anxious is at one end, next to him is the tall figure of Trusevich, the steadying influence on the team. The goalkeeper always looked calm, he relished the big occasion. His brother-in-law

Livshitz stands next to him along with the veteran Tyutchev, then Shylovsky and the gifted but erratic striker Komarov. Further down the line Nikolai Makhinya stares hard at the official photographer, with the look of a man who wants to dispense with a bothersome chore so he can get on with the real business of the day. The burly striker Ivan Kuzmenko is flanked on one side by Makhinya, on the other by Alexei Pravoverov. Kuzmenko, a man with a shot as powerful as it was accurate, stands with a half smile, possibly contemplating the game ahead. Towards the end of the line the young defender Klimenko looks anxious while, last in line, the bull-chested winger Makar Goncharenko is keenly anticipating the contest to come. At the end of the day it was, by all accounts, one of the best games seen in the Soviet Union until then. The two old rivals were closely matched in every department on the field and at the end of a fierce contest Dynamo of Moscow won by the only goal of the game. Moscow were champions and took the gold medal, having won all six of their games. Dynamo Kiev took a creditable silver medal position with Spartak, the only other team to beat them, coming third.

Kiev's other notable performance that year came when they faced the Turkish national side who were on a tour of the USSR. The game took place on 18 September in an appalling rainstorm, but Kiev were far too good for the Turks. Dynamo knew that the result would not be in doubt, so they tried to make it something of a show game. Trusevich was in goal only for the first half and Idzkovsky, who had seldom played since the French tour, came on for the second half, much to the delight of the crowd. In the end it scarcely mattered who was in goal since Kiev were dominant in every area of the game, beating the Turks 9–1. The game is probably more memorable for what happened afterwards. Trusevich was a man of impeccable manners and he felt that they had perhaps been less than hospitable by trouncing their guests 9–1, so he arranged an impromptu supper to cheer up the visitors. Both teams were there, the atmosphere was extremely cordial and Trusevich took it upon himself to provide the cabaret.

'He was very supple and strong,' his friend and rival Idzkovsky later recalled, 'and he would perform something called "The Dance of the Goalkeeper", which he did with a straight face.'

This comic turn from the goalkeeper began with an invitation to the band to strike up a medley of tangos or a jazz instrumental. Trusevich then began to bend and sway and throw himself around the hall as if in an imaginary goal area. He would stretch and leap to take a ball in the top right-hand corner, then he would swoop low to save an imaginary shot flying to his left. And all of this in time to the staccato rhythm of the music. The pièce de resistance came when the music stopped and Trusevich froze in the centre of the room. Suddenly he fell face forward. The crowd squealed with surprise as he headed towards the floor, but at the last minute he would put his arms down in front of him, drop into a push-up position, and then leap back to his feet. The crowd was delighted. The miserable weather and the humiliating result were forgotten as they called for encore after encore, which was the whole point of Trusevich's clowning. He obliged them time and time again. Each time he finished he would get to his feet, pull down his jacket, straighten his tie, and dust himself off before heading back to his seat to wait for the inevitable request for yet another reprise.

Trusevich was impeccable, fastidious and immaculately turned out in everything he did, but he was willing to lose his dignity for the sake of leaving the visitors with a happy memory of his team and his city. It was typical of the man. As a goalkeeper he was required to put himself in harm's way, which he did without complaint. Goalkeepers of that period were not given by the referee anything like the protection which their modern counterparts enjoy and Trusevich had more than his fair share of injuries. But there is no mention of him ever having complained or retaliated. However, if anyone were to step on his feet on the dance floor and spoil the shine on his gleaming patent shoes he would be thunderstruck. This was a constant source of amusement to his team-mates who never tired of trying to play practical jokes on him, but, with the same attitude that he brought to the football field, Trusevich never complained. Instead, he would simply bide his time until he could think of a way of paying them back.

Idzkovsky remembers him as being absolutely fearless and frequently willing to confuse opposition players by unexpectedly diving at their feet with no regard to his own safety. Similarly, unlike other keepers who preferred the security of their goal line, he would launch himself into the thick of a crowd of players to gather the ball.

'He was not invincible,' said Idzkovsky, 'but the strongest side of his character would not be seen until the dark days of the war.'

★

After that initial success in the first USSR championship, Dynamo Kiev finished third in the autumn championship of 1936. In subsequent years an increasing number of teams meant that it was no longer practical to have two tournaments and the league was decided in one championship which began in the spring and ended in the autumn. Dynamo came fifth in 1937 and fourth in 1938. In that 1938 championship, even though they were not among the top three, Dynamo Kiev set a new scoring record with seventy-six goals in a season. That year Dynamo's efforts were recognised when seven of their players – Nikolai Trusevich, Nikolai Makhinya, Nikolai Treber, Iosif Livshitz, Ivan Kuzmenko, Victor Shilovsky and Petr Laiko – were named in the list of the fifty-five best players in the Soviet Union.

By the time the 1939 championship came round the rest of Europe was preparing for war. In the Ukraine there was only a confident anticipation of another summer season of football. After their record goal-scoring performance in the previous year, the Kiev fans must have felt sure that their team could improve on that and possibly even win the championship. In fact they had a poor year, finishing out of the top places in a league that was won by Spartak Moscow. It was the same in 1940, when they were again unplaced as the Muscovite dominance continued with a win for Dynamo Moscow. There was no chance of Kiev improving their record in the 1941 tournament. The championship was suspended after only four games. Hitler's blitzkrieg had torn through Europe and now he was looking to the east.

# CHAPTER THREE

## 22 JUNE 1941

The thunder that the early-morning revellers mistakenly thought they could hear as they made their way home from the wedding was the rumble of German bombing raids sweeping towards the Ukraine at the start of Operation Barbarossa, the invasion of the Soviet Union. These were scenes which were repeated down the length of the Soviet Union's western border on that mid-summer morning as a German army of more than 3 million troops began its attack.

In 1941, despite all evidence to the contrary from almost everywhere else in Europe, Stalin still continued to put his faith in the much vaunted non-aggression pact with Germany. On 23 August 1939, he and his foreign minister, Vyacheslav Molotov, had personally met Joachim von Ribbentrop, Hitler's foreign minister, to sign the document which turned two ideological enemies into unlikely allies. The sincerity of both parties can be gauged by the fact that the swastikas and Nazi flags which adorned the signing ceremony had been scavenged from Soviet film studios where only months earlier they had been used in propaganda films demonising Hitler and all his works. Indeed, in 1938, as a crude way of inspiring national pride and inciting hatred against the Germans, Stalin had ordered the legendary Russian film-maker Sergei Eisenstein to make a film about the life of Alexander Nevsky. Stalin had even interfered with the script and ordered portions rewritten to show that Nevsky's thirteenth-century battle against the Teutonic Knights had very clear modern parallels. Not surprisingly, Eisenstein's film was withdrawn when the pact with Germany was signed.

There were practical and expedient reasons for both parties to sign the pact when they did. For Hitler, the signing of the pact deflected for the time being the prospect of any conflict in the east and bought him time to deal with the rest of Europe before turning his attention to what he knew was an inevitable ideological conflict with Bolshevism. For Stalin, the signing of the pact was an attempt to settle some old scores and reclaim former territories. The non-aggression pact allowed Hitler to invade Poland without fear of any reprisal from Russia. Germany invaded Poland one week after the signing of the pact and at the same time Stalin ordered the Soviet army to occupy and retake the province of Galicia. The unfortunate Poles were, therefore, caught between the swastika on one side as the German blitzkrieg poured in from the west, and Stalin's terror on the other as the dreaded NKVD – forerunners of the KGB – poured in from the east. Demarcation lines had already been agreed in advance and the Poles were the meat in a very bloody sandwich.

The non-aggression pact was nothing more than an elaborate sham. Three years previously Adolf Hitler had held a series of confidential briefings with some of his most trusted aides and advisers. In that summer of 1936 Hitler had spent a great deal of time at Berchtesgaden, his retreat in the Bavarian Alps. His mind had turned to war as he spent his summer days and nights plotting the future of his 1,000-year Reich. In particular, he had come to the conclusion that war between Germany and the Soviet Union was not only necessary but advisable. Bolshevism had to be crushed and Germany had to possess the might and the will to do it. Victory for the Russians, he believed, was unthinkable and would plunge Europe into a catastrophe which could take the continent back to the Dark Ages. Everything else from August 1936, when he drafted his secret memo on his future plans, was geared towards a military conflict with the Soviet Union. According to Hitler, the build-up in German military forces could not be too large or too quick. The head of the German air force, Hermann Goering, was put in charge of a Four-Year Plan, the aim of which was to have both the German military machine and the German economy ready for war within four years. As it happened, both were ready ahead of schedule.

Hitler had other more avaricious reasons for smashing the Soviet Union. Russia, he believed, could be to Germany what India had been to Britain. His doctrine of *Lebensraum*, or living space, claimed the Aryan master race needed room to grow. Hitler had visions of a swift conquest of the Soviet Union, which would allow him to plunder the country for its natural resources needed to pursue the war elsewhere. His Eastern Empire would be a haven for his new ruling class, who were seduced with the thought of villas by the Black Sea and a life of ease and plenty with a broken local population as a servile underclass. Negotiations with Stalin were little more than a charade. Hitler had no intention of permanently observing any kind of non-aggression pact, but it suited his purposes to have Stalin believe that he would. Hitler even went so far as to sign the Tripartite Pact with Italy and Japan which, in 1940, effectively carved up the world between the three nations. He then used this pact to bait his hook for Stalin by inviting him to join the agreement a few weeks later. But while von Ribbentrop shuttled between Berlin and Moscow, Hitler's plans continued without halt or hesitation as Operation Barbarossa inexorably took shape in secret. In May 1941, there were nine German armies totalling 150 divisions arrayed around the Soviet borders. There were almost 200 incursions into Soviet air space as the Luftwaffe flew reconnaissance missions over their chosen targets.

Superficially Stalin may have been pleased with what he had managed to acquire with the non-aggression pact. He had gained large amounts of territory with scarcely a shot fired; in addition he had, or so he believed, reached an accommodation with a potential enemy. In reality, both sides had won themselves a little time. Besides, in 1939, neither Germany nor the Soviet Union was prepared for a war against the other. Hitler's conquest of Western Europe was played out on the battlefields of France, Czechoslovakia, Poland, Scandinavia, and the Low Countries. All toppled under the Nazi blitzkrieg.

But communism, or more specifically Bolshevism, remained anathema. For one thing Hitler saw it as being a Semitic plot. So many saw the war in the east as inevitable but Stalin, seemingly, was not one of them. Whatever suspicions he may have harboured, Stalin honoured the terms of the Molotov–von Ribbentrop pact, which provided that Russia would supply Germany with essential raw materials. His advisers told him Hitler would invade. Richard Sorge, a German communist spy based in Tokyo and one of the Soviet Union's most brilliant intelligence agents, told him Hitler would invade. Not only did Sorge tell Stalin that Hitler would invade, he told him where and when, even though he gave the date as 20 June 1941. Even the British informed Stalin that Hitler would invade. Stalin ignored them all. On 21 June, the massed German units received the code word 'Dortmund' telling them that the attack would start in the early hours of the following day. A Wehrmacht soldier with communist sympathies deserted and crossed over to the Soviet lines with the news. The unfortunate man was shot on Stalin's instructions.

At three o'clock in the morning of 22 June 1941, German guns opened up on unprepared Soviet positions. Operation Barbarossa – the code name given to Hitler's plan for the conquest and subjugation of the Soviet Union – had begun. Three hours later, Muscovites awoke to a normal Sunday. The radio played music for their physical exercises and there was no mention of the invasion. Indeed, the invasion was not mentioned until the lunchtime news bulletins, nine hours after the barrage had begun, by which time German troops were already on Soviet soil and striking deeper and deeper into Russian territory. Initially, the Germans were literally unopposed, messages coming back from Moscow told Soviet gunners that Stalin had forbidden them to return fire on the German batteries. Thousands of ill-equipped and poorly-led Soviet troops died where they stood, the Russian air force was bombed ruthlessly without ever getting off the ground – one German pilot described it as 'infanticide' – and unsuspecting Soviet citizens, who had trusted Stalin in this as they had in all things, perished without ever understanding he had been so fatally and spectacularly wrong. Stalin's response was to take to his dacha in the country for two days where he had a minor breakdown while the German blitzkrieg stormed across his country.

Konstantin Shchegotsky could not believe what he had heard when he took the call telling him the war had started. This was supposed to be a special day for Dynamo Kiev. They were to open the new Republic Sports Stadium that afternoon. This was where the wedding party guests had arranged to meet up. It was to be a huge celebration with gymnastics, boxing matches and a football game between Kiev and CDKA, the army team, a side which was destined to vanish in the conflict to come. Shchegotsky could not take it all in. They had been on the pitch the previous day, they had kicked a ball around on the turf and commented to each other about how good the surface was. The players were impressed with the stadium and the pitch. They were looking forward to the game. Butusov the coach had even named his team a day early. Shchegotsky was playing, so was Makhinya, and, of course, Trusevich was in goal.

In keeping with his relaxed appearance and

impeccable manners, Trusevich was not the sort of player to get terribly nervous before a game, even a big game. The match against CDKA, the team which later became better known as CSKA, was not a big game. There was nothing at stake, no championships or trophies would be decided. But it was an event. There would be a big crowd, and Trusevich was confident that he would not let anyone down. Even so, he had trouble sleeping that night. He, too, was wakened by the strange sounds which he took to be distant thunder. He gave up trying to get back to sleep and finally roused himself around four, sitting quietly in the living room of their small apartment while his wife Lyolya and his little daughter Svetlana slept next door. He went to the window and saw that the sky outside was blue and peaceful with the merest hint of pink as the new day dawned. There was no sign of the thunderstorm which he believed had wakened him. Trusevich decided to dress and go out for some fresh air. He walked down the two flights of stairs on to Kreschatinski Lane and found the janitor of the building hosing down the pavement while glancing nervously at the sky from time to time.

'They say a war has started,' the janitor said.

'Who says?' asked Trusevich.

'Someone in apartment six had a visitor, a soldier who asked him to go to the drafting point,' said the janitor, still looking nervously up at the brightening sky.

Trusevich quickly returned upstairs. He woke his wife and told her what he had learned from the janitor. After warning her to stay in the house, he went to meet the rest of the team. Konstantin Shchegotsky had come to the same conclusion after his early morning call. He was entitled to an apartment, but he had given it up to a married team-mate because he thought it was wasteful for a single man to be staying in a flat which could be put to better use. Shchegotsky now lived in a hotel and once for himself he heard the explosions in the distance, he decided to go and meet his team-mates. He dressed quickly, ran downstairs, and headed for the Continental Hotel just a few streets away. The Continental was where Mikhail Pavlovich Butusov lived permanently with his family. As he expected, Shchegotsky found his trainer in the hotel lobby when he arrived. The two men had a brief conversation but neither was any the wiser and in the end they decided to go directly to the Dynamo Stadium. Although the news was spreading that the war had started there was surprisingly little panic in the streets. No one yet knew what the war would bring and how soon it would reach them. People stood in small groups trying to come to terms with what was happening. There were concerned conversations in parks and courtyards, but no one could really offer an explanation or confirm facts. Eventually the anti-aircraft batteries did open up, but they were firing far too high to have any effect on the German aircraft. Vadim Sinyavsky, a Moscow Radio journalist who was a friend of Shchegotsky and had come to Kiev to commentate on the big match, instead found himself lying on a window ledge at the Continental filing some of the earliest eyewitness accounts from the beginning of the war as the German bombs fell on the outskirts of the city. Kiev, Odessa and Lviv were all bombed on the first day of Operation Barbarossa.

Almost to a man, the other Dynamo players had headed to their stadium. By the time Trusevich reached it almost everyone else had already arrived, including Butusov. They too did not know quite what to do. Like everywhere else in Kiev the atmosphere was one of quiet incredulity, they simply could not believe that a war had begun, nor could they understand why. The players were still ready to play, but once they heard Molotov finally announce on the radio that war had been declared, they recognised there would be no game that afternoon. They stayed at the ground until three – the match was supposed to kick off at five – then, realising there was little else to be done, they drifted away and returned to their homes and families.

When he launched Operation Barbarossa Hitler had every belief that the Bolsheviks would be defeated and the Soviet Union conquered by Christmas. Certainly in the first few weeks of the campaign he had seen or heard nothing to convince him that the calculations of his generals and advisers were anything other than completely accurate. Three million men attacked along a front 1,800 kilometres wide, the longest in history. Army Group North under Field Marshal von Leeb drove towards Leningrad and the Baltic States, Field Marshal von Bock and his Army Group Centre attacked Minsk, Smolensk and ultimately would push ahead to the outskirts of Moscow itself, while Army Group South commanded by Field Marshal von Runstedt swarmed towards the Ukraine. By the middle of July, Bialystok, Minsk and Smolensk had been captured. Minsk fell on the ninth day of the campaign, Smolensk fell two weeks later. Barbarossa was less than a month old and already the Germans had taken a million prisoners and were only 200 miles from Moscow. The gently undulating steppe, which had proved so welcoming and unobstructive to would-be conquerors for centuries, proved even easier to negotiate for the onrushing Panzer divisions. The invading German soldiers joked that the only serious problem they had encountered was the choking clouds of dust which were being thrown up by the tanks in the vanguard of the invasion. In the hot summer without a breath of wind, these plumes of dust hung in the sky like ribbons marking the astonishing progress of the German troops. But just when the whole of the Soviet Union seemed at his mercy, instead of pressing on to Moscow, Hitler decided to head for the wheatfields of the Ukraine and the oil fields of the Black Sea. Although at the time this was seen as a bizarre decision, events in Stalingrad later would prove that Hitler was perhaps right not to risk the prospect of his armies becoming bogged down at Moscow. Even so, this unanticipated drive south towards the Ukraine – and Kiev – was not expected by the Germans to slow their progress significantly.

# CHAPTER FOUR

When it was evident the German army had begun to cross the Russian borders, Ukrainians, fiercely proud of their homeland, rushed to the recruiting offices in droves to enlist. Nikolai Trusevich's reaction was typical of Kiev as a whole. He went to volunteer for the army on 23 June, the day after Hitler had launched the invasion. At the recruiting office, prepared to do his patriotic duty, Trusevich was informed of what many of the other volunteers had already been told: the Red Army would take care of the invaders and sweep the Motherland clean.

The bullish mood of the recruiting officer was reflected in the rest of the city. Although the Soviet Union was at war, apart from that initial air raid, so far Kiev and its environs were not apparently affected and day-to-day life in Kiev was largely unaltered. For the following few days the people of Kiev went about their business as usual. No one cancelled travel arrangements, people did not change their plans, and there was an air of fragile bonhomie in the city. The cinemas were still full, the cafés and restaurants were busy and, according to a local newspaper, *Proletarskaya Pravda,* department stores in Kiev were selling between 400,000 and 500,000 roubles worth of goods every day. The average monthly wage at this time was between 50 and 100 roubles. It is difficult to reconcile these statistics. This may have been a spending spree brought on by subconscious fears that the tranquil life would not last, but it seems more likely that it was a crude propaganda attempt to deflect attention away from the gravity of the situation. Defeatist talk, though, was discouraged at every turn. Everyone expected the war to end very soon and the newspaper headlines screamed out slogans such as 'We will kill the enemy where we find him'.

Within the following few weeks the mood in Kiev changed, at first slowly, then abruptly. The newspapers, which were little more than mouthpieces for the Communist Party. started to change the tone of their headlines. Soon they were declaring 'Eliminate spies and saboteurs' and 'Death to panic-mongers'. Exhortation had been replaced by increasingly shrill and authoritarian threats. Rumours abounded. When the first consignment of wounded was brought into Kiev from a town to the west where the fighting was heavy, the news quickly spread through the city along with the fiction that the injured were all Pioneers – young children – whose train had been bombed by the Germans. Again this appears to have been propaganda. The wounded were most likely civilian and military casualties from the rapidly-advancing German front, whose arrival could not have done much for the confidence of the Kievans. There were also whispers that the city administration had given up and fled, which turned out not to be true, although they would leave the city later and relocate to Ufa in Siberia. None of the tales was accurate but together they marked a perceptible shift in tone, emphasised by the beginning of a programme of mass evacuation of key industrial workers to the comparative safety of the Urals in the east, away from the front. Each industrial sector was given its own time and date for evacuation and although the operation was well organised an air of barely-suppressed panic hung over the railway station. The bakery workers were due to be evacuated by special train on 6 July. Valentina Dubovsky, married for less than three weeks, was being sent away with her workmates but Alexei was to remain in the city where his engineering skills would be needed. She and her friends baked a whole carriage load of fresh bread for the journey and Valentina and Alexei tried to make light of it as they kissed farewell. But theirs was not, as they had been led to believe, a temporary separation. Alexei would stay and be killed in the defence of the city. Valentina was evacuated to safety but, after the war, when she learned of Alexei's death she could not bring herself to return to Kiev and lived out her days instead in distant Tashkent.

The Germans pushed further and further eastwards into the heart of the Soviet Union. They were using their normal battle strategy. The tank divisions would punch a hole through the opposing lines, then infantry divisions would move out in a huge circle right and left to flank the enemy while the tanks and armoured divisions poured through this single narrow gap. These encircling tactics had already worked to devastating effect throughout Russia and there was no sign that they would fail in the

Ukraine. The Ukrainians fought desperately but after a while, when it became clear that they could not repulse the invaders, the preferred option was merely to break out of the encirclement so that they could regroup and fight again. Many Kievans were able to break out into the woods and forests where they joined partisan groups to harry the Germans wherever they could.

Kiev found itself in a constant state of agitation and the civil authorities began to take a tighter and tighter grip. The evacuation campaign intensified. Sports clubs in the Soviet Union were an integral part of the community and provided a whole range of services. Not surprisingly Dynamo's stadium became a focal point for the evacuation operation. Some of the Dynamo players such as Trusevich, Makhinya and Kuzmenko did eventually join the military, while others remained in Kiev. Some who had played for Dynamo in years past were too old for military service, others chose to stay and tend to their families. Konstantin Shchegotsky, for example, was excused active duty because, at his medical in June, he was still suffering from the effects of a painful skin complaint. He stayed at the Dynamo stadium and helped to organise the evacuation, as he recalled later in a memoir.

It was, he said, a poignant time, full of old friends bidding farewell to one another, possibly for the last time. Butusov's family had departed, so had the goalkeeper Idzkovsky's family, and the striker Komarov also managed to get his wife and daughter out. Shchegotsky persuaded his own daughter and his ex-wife to leave, Trusevich's wife – Livshitz's sister – and her daughter also went, reaching the relative safety of

Odessa on the Black Sea coast. Those who remained, in a valiant pretence of normality, managed to keep open all the sports facilities at the stadium as well as the club shop in Kreschatik Street.

By the end of August 1941, Kiev was almost within the grasp of the German army. The 37th Red Army had fought desperately, but lacking guns and ammunition it was hopeless. The army itself was a mixture of regular soldiers and inexperienced citizens' militia, comprised mostly of men who were too old for military service and boys who were too young. They were pathetically ill-equipped and at times had scarcely more than one rifle between five men, with hardly any ammunition for the shared weapon. Many of the experienced officers had been purged by Stalin during the Terror of the thirties. The Red Army could not hope to hold out for long against the relentless drive of the German Panzers. The Germans very quickly took the villages which covered the high ground on the main road into Kiev from Moscow in the north-west. From there they could control the battlefield and move at their own pace. For the Soviet army it was imperative that this road be kept open. If the Germans took control of this main artery then Kiev would be cut off by the German encirclement and would almost certainly fall. The Red Army had fought frantically to defend the north road and having lost it they fought even more desperately to get it back. The battle-hardened German troops were astonished at the efforts which the Russians were prepared to make to retake the road and even more astonished at the tactics they were prepared to employ. An infantry division of the German 6th Army, the army that would be lost in

Stalingrad two years later, was in charge of the high ground and they had to withstand three days of Soviet counter-attacks, including the terrors of night attacks, a taste of the terrible, obdurate street fighting to come.

By taking control of the high ground above the road the Germans had an uninterrupted field of fire for miles around. Any attempt to attack the German positions was tantamount to suicide unless conducted in force with daring, imagination and extraordinarily well-drilled troops. The Red Army had vast amounts of troops but was lacking in all of the other qualities and their onslaught was therefore doomed. The counter-attacks generally began with an artillery barrage, which was usually laid down so inaccurately that little or no damage was done to the German positions. The Germans could laugh off the inefficiency of the Soviet gunners, but the tenacity and ferocity of the Russian infantrymen genuinely terrified them. One experienced German soldier, who had withstood counter-attacks during earlier fighting in France, could not believe what he was seeing when the Russians attacked. According to his eyewitness account the brown-uniformed men began to march forward in wave after wave. Each rank was separated by about 200 metres from the one in front. The Germans watched fascinated as they crossed a small river at the bottom of the hill and marched stolidly up the slope towards them. Once the artillery barrage had started, the German commander had brought all of his machine guns and automatic weapons into the line in anticipation of a Soviet attack. As the Russians continued their march up the hill, the Germans had nothing to do but take aim and wait.

At 600 metres the German commanding officer gave

the order to fire and the first wave of Soviet troops simply disappeared, cut down like the wheat in the fields through which they had tramped. There were one or two who had survived the fusillade by sheer luck, but rather than turn or seek cover they kept on marching, arming themselves with the weapons of their fallen comrades. This spirit is what shocked the Germans more than anything, the notion that men with only a few rounds of ammunition would continue to advance in such carnage shook them to the core. Two hundred metres behind the first rank, the second wave advanced. By this stage these were men who plainly knew what was in front of them but were driven on by a fierce determination to sweep the invaders from their land and reclaim their country. The second wave disappeared as quickly and as pointlessly as the first, and the third wave after that, and then the fourth wave. The fourth wave presented an even easier target since they could barely find space to march across the bodies of their dead comrades. The German fire was continuous and relentless. The only break in the shooting came when the barrels of the machine guns became red hot with use and had to be cooled. Still the Soviet troops came on. Finally, they forsook their formation and attacked in a mass, but the German firepower was too great. Ultimately the Soviets broke and retreated down the hill without having inflicted any significant casualties on the German lines. Even in the face of such appalling carnage there was no respite for either side. Within an hour the Soviets were back on the attack with another five waves of men. When that was repulsed in similar fashion to the first, they waited an hour and sent in a third attack and still another one after that.

German soldiers were horrified at the devastation they were inflicting. They pitied their opponents for their lack of leadership at the same time as they admired their raw courage. The Russians seemed to be using tactics which had been determined by their political commissars and not their officers. These were tactics which dated from the Revolution and appeared to have been decided by mathematical formulae rather than military experience. The commissars, so the Germans insisted, worked out the number of machine guns their men would face multiplied by the number of rounds they could fire in a minute. They then worked out how long it would take a certain number of soldiers to cross a given area of ground. Having come up with a likely attrition figure they then added on a few thousand to ensure that at least some got through.

The Germans on the hill were both astonished at the ease of their victory and at the same time awestruck by the determination of the Soviet troops. No German soldier would continue to advance on his own, but here were Soviet troops continuing to march up a hill, slipping in their comrades' blood, while thousands of men were slaughtered right and left of them. There was no hint that anyone was preparing to turn and run. These men were fighting without the incentive of the blocking divisions Stalin would later employ at Moscow. These blocking divisions, usually from the despised NKVD, were there purely and simply to stiffen the resolve of the Soviet troops by shooting anyone who retreated from the front and came in their direction. But there were no blocking divisions on the high ground above the Kiev road. Some other force had driven the

Soviet army on. Since the Revolution one thing, and one thing above all, had been drummed into the minds of all Russians. Whether they had learned it through the bitter lessons of the Revolution or whether they learned it mantra-like in school, they knew that the Motherland was all they had and they should defend it with their lives. The 37th Red Army had no choice but to fight.

The Red Army kept up this succession of murderous and ruinous counter-attacks for three days before they finally withdrew, leaving the Germans to advance uninterrupted. But even as they moved inexorably towards Kiev, the invading Germans took with them a new sense of the real fight ahead. Hitler and his general staff might fill the airwaves with stirring hyperbole about the imminent defeat of the Soviet Union, but the rank and file soldiers began to understand that the war in Russia was not going to turn out to be as easy as everyone was suggesting.

Operation Barbarossa also showed the NKVD at its most brutal. Eyewitness accounts from German soldiers tell of the carnage they discovered as the NKVD retreated before them along with the remnants of the Red Army and the citizens' militias. In some cases the NKVD evacuated its prisoners to relatively safer areas further east. But in other cases where they were being overrun or where they simply felt inclined, they slaughtered the incarcerated in their cells. In Lviv, for example, there were several thousand prisoners, mostly Ukrainian nationalists, being held in three separate prisons. When the Germans overran the city on 29 June they did not find a single prisoner left alive. Instead they found piles of bodies, sometimes five deep. The NKVD had simply machine-gunned them in their cells and then fled before the arrival of the advancing Germans.

Leon Weliczer, now a writer, was sixteen years old when Lviv came under attack. Three days after the city had fallen to the Nazis, he and his father were taken by Ukrainian militia who were determined to avenge the deaths of their nationalist comrades. For three days what became known as the Lviv Massacre went on without a break. Jews were rounded up and clubbed to death by Ukrainian militia, who were anti-Semitic. They were lined up face down on a hockey pitch, then chosen one at a time. Those who were selected were chased round the field by truncheon-wielding militia and beaten to death. Weliczer recalls lapsing into unconsciousness at one point, only to wake later to find himself lying next to two men whose skulls had been shattered by clubs. By the end of the third day, more than 2,000 people had been slaughtered.

As the Germans approached Kiev, the footballers were part of the desperate struggle to save the city and to protect their families. By 1 September the Germans were only a few miles from the city and the situation was becoming more obviously acute. As the Germans advanced and the Red Army and the citizens' militias did what they could to keep them at bay, Shchegotsky and his colleagues turned to more active duties. They had been helping to clothe and equip the NKVD officers, who were fighting their way out of the city to join the partisans in the woods to continue a guerrilla war against the invaders. They also served double duty as volunteer firemen trying to control the damage done by German bombs and shells. With the Red Army descending further and further into chaos, the partisans played a more active role in the defence of the city. The partisan headquarters in the Ukraine was based in the incongruously named Tom Sawyer cinema not far from the Dynamo Stadium. Deputy Minister of Internal Affairs Timofei Strokach was in charge of the partisan operation as well as being the head of the Republican Council of Dynamo Teams. Strokach realised that with all of the roads now controlled by the Germans, the Dnieper remained their only possible lifeline. Strokach had a barge loaded with artwork, icons, jewellery and other valuables and commandeered an out-of-service submarine to tow it south-east along the Dnieper as far as Dniepropetrovsk some 200 miles away. Even while he was organising all of this, Strokach also took the time to make sure that none of Dynamo's trophies or mementoes would fall into German hands. He arranged to have them smuggled out of the city to safety as well.

These barges on the Dnieper also represented the last hope of some of the remaining Dynamo players and their families. The club provided a hostel next to the stadium where players from all over western Ukraine stayed during their training sessions with Kiev. Strokach ordered those players who were left to gather their wives and families and go with the barges. It was plain to anyone that the city could not survive for much longer. Privately some of the older members of the Dynamo Kiev side wondered what would happen to them if they remained in Kiev. They knew that the prevailing propaganda in some quarters was that life under Hitler had to be better than life under Stalin, but they were not wholly convinced. The senior players such as Idzkovsky and Shchegotsky had recognised that while, before the war, the club's sponsorship by the NKVD was frequently a desirable thing, it could work against them now. Where previously they had the protection of the NKVD umbrella, if the city fell they would be regarded as implacable enemies of the new rulers. They understood that there might be no room for compromise as far as the Germans were concerned. And so Butusov and Shchegotsky went to Lev Varnavsky, the head of the NKVD in Kiev, to ask for his help. The families of the players were already being evacuated from the city, but they asked that the players themselves and the remainder of the club officials be evacuated as well for their own safety. Varnavsky simply accused them of cowardice and rejected their request out of hand. Later Varnavsky would be one of the first to be shot by the Germans on the very day that they took over the city.

Despite the official refusal some players managed to leave with their families, but most sent their wives and children and stayed behind to defend the city. The Dynamo players who were not in the regular army were put under the command of a special citizens' committee which, as it happened, included Konstantin Shchegotsky. The barges on which Strokach set such store began the hazardous journey along the Dnieper at the beginning of September. The Germans were pounding the Dnieper fleet and the barges could only get as far as Cherkasy, scarcely more secure than Kiev and less than halfway to Dniepropetrovsk. The end for Kiev was only a matter of days away now. The constant sound of artillery and gunfire seemed to come closer and closer by the hour. Eventually the Germans were inside the suburbs. The partisans and militia men fought an increasingly hopeless fight. They battled street by street, house by house, metre by metre. Nikolai Makhinya was one of many who distinguished himself. He led a small band of soldiers who harried and fought the Germans with a savagery that scarcely concealed their despair.

Nikolai Makhinya had been a passionate Stalinist all his life. He was the head of a platoon which fought for Kiev to the end. By mid-September Makhinya was in charge of no more than a few men. It was a mixed unit of regulars and militia but, despite their lack of numbers and even more acute lack of equipment, still they would not surrender. They continued to fight in an effort to escape the rapidly-closing encirclement. Makhinya was inspirational: his comrades remember him attacking the Germans while screaming pro-Stalinist slogans. But as the fighting wore on he realised that the battle was lost. He and his men never had enough food, or enough ammunition, or enough of anything. When they inspected the bodies of the Germans they killed they saw soldiers who were well-fed, well-equipped, and had fought in a well-disciplined manner. They even had maps of the Ukraine, which was something the defending forces were desperately lacking. The Soviet shore batteries along the Dnieper may have sent up thousands of shells but the German Junkers dive-bombers flew too low for the Russian barrage to have any effect. The Soviet gunners, too, were poorly trained and poorly equipped. One Junkers was, on average, able to take out five of its Russian counterparts. Makhinya and his remaining troops fought out of desperate instinct. There was no command structure and when officers could be found to issue orders they frequently contradicted each other. Makhinya had spent twenty days trying to lead his men out of the encirclement but could not. He had lived all his life in Kiev. He had been born and raised in Podol, the most ancient part of the city, a beautiful warren of churches and back streets. His father was a river boatman who had fought on the Volga during the First World War and on the Dnieper in the Civil War. Now Nikolai had no option but to take his men back into his city and defend it with their lives.

As the battle for Kiev reached its climax, Stalin ordered a motivational speech to be played to the men and women in the trenches. The heroism and determination of these valiant defenders cannot be underestimated. Badly led and poorly equipped, they stood their ground and died at their posts and for many of them the last thing they heard was the tinny sound of Stalin's voice exhorting them not to give up a single foot of territory. As they advanced the Germans had the bizarre experience of overrunning positions from which Stalin's 'morale-boosting' speech was still being played over the tannoy. As the fate of Kiev became obvious, the Soviet commanders begged Stalin to surrender the city so that the troops might withdraw and regroup. Instead, in increasingly fanatical tones, they were urged to repel the invaders with everything at their disposal. The Soviet commander Marshal Sukharev, who would become one of the greatest commanders of the Second World War, told Stalin that the city could not be saved and was dismissed from his post, a demotion he was not unhappy to accept under the circumstances. The Kievans, who deserved better than they had ever received from Stalin, responded with savage ferocity. They were not though, in their hearts, fighting for the Soviet motherland, they were fighting for the Ukraine. Every farmhouse, every village, every crossroads was defended to the death.

In the city itself there was no such thing as a non-combatant. Everyone rallied to defend Kiev from the invaders. As the Germans approached and entered the outskirts of the city what had once been a long-range war of tanks and artillery became a bloody close-quarters conflict of mines and booby-traps, and after that of knives and clubs and whatever weapons came to hand. The entire remaining population joined in the resistance. Many of the snipers, for example, were women and they fought with devastating effect. One of the most famous, who fought in other parts of the Ukraine, was Major Ludmila Pavlychenko. She was so successful with her 309 credited kills that she was used on propaganda tours to other Allied countries to win support for Russia against Germany. She was fortunate: she was able to escape. Others had to stay and fight. Konstantin Shchegotsky may have been the darling of the intelligentsia but when the shells and bombs began to fall inside the city, he, too, became a soldier. As the Germans came closer and closer to the city, Shchegotsky gave up his duties as a volunteer fireman as he and the rest of his comrades were ordered to join a military unit.

Kiev finally fell on 19 September 1941. The city had been set alight by the Germans and the Russians. The high explosives and incendiary devices of the advancing Germans had played their part in setting fire to the city; encouraged by Stalin's exhortations to employ a scorched earth policy leaving nothing for the invaders, the Russians did the rest. The Dniprohes Dam on the Dnieper was the largest hydro-electric dam in Europe, but the Soviets destroyed it rather than leave it for the Germans. Every major factory which could be reached was rigged with explosives and destroyed along with every fuel dump, every warehouse, and anything else which might be useful to the invading army. It was broad daylight when the Germans entered the city, but the sky was thick with black clouds of smoke that hung like a shroud over the city blotting out the sun. The eclipse which had been forecast for two days later seemed to have come early.

Nikolai Makhinya wept with anger and shame when he saw his beloved city burning like a torch. The night before Makhinya had gone to sleep knowing that all was lost. When he awoke on the morning of 19 September his friends swear his hair had turned grey from grief overnight.

Just before the city finally capitulated, Shchegotsky and another Kiev player Yatchmennikov, a reserve goalkeeper, were astonished to find Kolya Trusevich at the stadium. He was wounded and he was with a group of starving companions. Shchegotsky barely recognised his old friend. Only a scar on his left cheek – a souvenir of a training ground accident when he and Livshitz had been going for the same ball – gave him away. Trusevich the perennial joker was now, according to Shchegotsky, melancholy and depressed. He knew that the struggle for Kiev was in its death throes and the Germans could not be halted. Shchegotsky and Yatchmennikov treated Trusevich and his friends as best they could as they exchanged war stories. Trusevich, a lithe and graceful athlete, had found himself using his talents in perilous missions behind the enemy lines. He had on several occasions slipped behind the German front and returned with a prisoner for interrogation.

One morning a few days earlier, Trusevich had been based with his unit in the Goloseyevsky Forest near Kiev. Under cover of the early morning mist and fog which clung to the forest ravines, he and four others went out on a scouting mission and found themselves close to a German foxhole. Hidden behind a thick clump of ferns, they could see the Germans dozing at their posts. Trusevich spotted one soldier with a machine gun who was supposed to be on guard. He appeared to be nodding off, while another, whose head Trusevich could see sticking out of the trench, appeared to have already fallen fast asleep with his grey forage cap over his eyes. These two might provide valuable information under interrogation. Quickly he asked for a volunteer and when one of the others, a particularly large and powerful soldier, offered his services, the two of them slipped out from behind the bushes. The two men crawled forward and picked their targets. Trusevich went for the sleeping soldier and swiftly flipped him face down, gagged him and started to tie him up. The other Russian went for the guard at the machine gun, but before he could gag him the German started screaming and yelling. Trusevich hoisted his prisoner on to his shoulder and started to make for cover. The other Russian did the same, but by this time the remaining Germans had awoken and were reaching for their weapons. Trusevich did his best to sprint back to his own men as the Germans opened fire. He looked back in time to see the other Russian fall to the ground, dead. His prisoner also appeared to have been killed by the indiscriminate shooting of his own men. As he made for the depths of the forest Trusevich felt a burning pain below his knee: he had been shot and could hardly use one leg. He struggled forward to be met by the other three Russians who had come up to help. One of them grabbed Nikolai, the other two grabbed the German beneath the arms and they dragged them both towards the woods. The Germans meanwhile began to mount a mortar barrage towards the Russians, forcing them deeper and deeper into the forest and further away from their own troops. Trusevich and the others struggled desperately to get back to Soviet lines. By the time he reached the relative safety of the Soviet troops it was evening. He had spent the day wounded and hunted in the forest, both prisoners were dead and only two of his colleagues, both badly injured, made it back with him.

The Germans came at them in strength in the morning and, wounded though he was, Trusevich was back in the Soviet trenches doing his best to repulse another German attack. They could not hold out for long and two days later he was wounded again. All this occurred barely a week before he was discovered by Shchegotsky and Yatchmennikov. Now Trusevich was struggling to stay alive and continue the fight by joining whatever makeshift unit he could find. Shchegotsky and Yatchmennikov shared what little food and water they had with him and his weary comrades. They also scraped together enough clean rags to dress their wounds before they went on their way again. At the gates of the stadium Trusevich turned and embraced both Shchegotsky and

Yatchmennikov and left without a word. The following day, 19 September 1941, Kiev was at last conceded to the Germans. Stalin, who had ordered that the city be defended at all costs, realised that protecting Kiev could mean losing Moscow. He finally accepted that the city would have to be abandoned to the Germans for the sake of the rest of the Soviet Union.

'Yachek and I were ordered to leave Kiev,' remembered Shchegotsky. 'We said goodbye to football in our own way. We took a couple of footballs and went out on to the field for about ten minutes. Yachek went in goal and we had a kick around. Then we sat on the benches remembering the friends with whom we had spent so much time there. It was a glorious summer, an Indian summer at its best, and I remember we desperately wanted time to stand still.'

As he left the Dynamo stadium Shchegotsky turned his back on a host of memories of his days in the team and in the city. His farewell was especially poignant. The other Dynamo players had been more than team-mates to him. On one occasion three years earlier in the confused paranoia of Stalin's purges, Shchegotsky had owed his life to his team-mates at Dynamo.

Shchegotsky, who had once been arrested for not wearing the state decoration which had still to be presented to him, was finally invested at a ceremony in the George Hall of the Kremlin in June 1938. Although he had promised to wear his award proudly, he was scarcely given the opportunity. Dynamo Kiev's next game was at home against Leningrad. After the match, as he was getting ready to go back to his hotel, two men approached him. They claimed to work for the NKVD and asked him if he would mind coming for a talk with their superiors. Shchegotsky was taken to NKVD headquarters in Institutskaya Street where he was formally denounced as an enemy of the people. There was scarcely a more serious accusation which could be levied at a Soviet citizen. In later years, men such as Alexander Solzhenitsyn and Andrei Sakharov, whose persecution would make their names known around the world, were punished for the very crime of which Shchegotsky was now being accused. The 27-year-old footballer would spend more than a year as a prisoner in the building while the NKVD attempted to prove a case against him. In a memoir published later Shchegotsky recalled how there were 106 people in his cell and 94 of them had state decorations just like his. These were doctors, teachers, scientists and engineers – all of them Bolsheviks who had joined the Party before the Revolution.

Shchegotsky was taken to Room 21 on the fourth floor of the building where he was tortured for twelve days. The favoured tactic of the interrogators was a technique called 'The Conveyor', which was a crude form of psychological assault. The unfortunate victim would be interrogated non-stop by a succession of interviewers, one after the other, until the prisoner was so confused he would agree to anything. But the Conveyor came after the victim had been softened up by physical torture. Shchegotsky was beaten nearly senseless with chair legs, as well as having his fingers broken – one by one – in the jamb of the solid oak door of the interrogation room. All they wanted, his accusers said, was for him to agree that he was a spy. Shchegotsky refused again and again. He was sustained by his fellow prisoners who, when he was thrown back into the cell after each session, told him that he must find a way of coping with everything. He must never agree to anything, he must not condemn himself out of his own mouth.

The core of the NKVD case rested on the rumour, which despite his straitened childhood circumstances was apparently true, that Shchegotsky was the son of a Polish nobleman. He had gone to Turkey to play as a member of the USSR team which went there in 1936. This, they believed, meant that he was almost certainly a Polish or Turkish spy. The paranoid logic of Konstantin Shchegotsky's case was multiplied across the thousands of other victims of the Terror. So determined were the NKVD to convict Shchegotsky that they brought in his team-mates and interrogated them too. None of them was tortured but they were questioned forcefully and made to sign papers refusing to reveal what they had seen or heard in the NKVD building. Many of the players kept their vow of silence and it was not until the era of glasnost in the days of Mikhail Gorbachev that the story of the team's interrogation finally came to light. Those who were still alive then admitted that the NKVD had been very persuasive and determined in their attempts to brand Shchegotsky as a spy. But none of his team-mates would give evidence against him.

Nikolai Makhinya, perhaps more than most, had good reason to dislike Shchegotsky. If Shchegotsky was guilty of even part of what he was accused, then he was the antithesis of everything the hard-line Stalinist Makhinya believed in. Makhinya's NKVD interrogators kept pressuring him and bringing up his own proletarian background, pointing out that he should not be supporting a Polish spy who was doing his best to usurp the authority of the team's trainers. Shchegotsky, as befitted his cavalier attitude to life, was not the best of trainers, but there was no evidence to suggest he was trying to subvert, still less supplant the team's coaches. Makhinya was repeatedly asked what sort of unusual things he noticed about his team-mate. Finally, he was confronted with the bald accusation: Shchegotsky was a spy for Poland. Makhinya's only response was to burst out laughing. Makhinya actually feared for himself after his reaction, but he told his interrogators that he honestly could not believe that his team-mate was a spy. He told them that he did not approve of the way Shchegotsky lived his life and he was especially scathing of his weaknesses – the smoking, the drinking and the womanising – but he could not believe he was anything other than a good and honest Soviet citizen who was very useful to the country as a football player.

It took Konstantin Shchegotsky fifteen months to escape from the clutches of the NKVD. In the end he had two strokes of luck. The first, and most telling, was that there was not a shred of evidence against him and no one could be found among his team-mates who would denounce him, no matter what the consequences to themselves. His second piece of luck came when Nikolai Yezhov was removed as head of the NKVD on 8 December 1938. In a moment of supreme neurosis Yezhov was himself later denounced as an enemy of the people and executed. The new head of the NKVD was Lavrenti Beria who immediately blamed Yezhov for having been too harsh and having wielded his powers in far too draconian a manner. During his own tenure Beria would resort to all of Yezhov's extremes, but in the early days at least he was willing to grant a number of amnesties and Shchegotsky was one of the fortunate who were allowed to go free.

Konstantin Shchegotsky was released from the NKVD prison in the autumn of 1939. Physically he was in such poor shape and his legs were so swollen that he could barely walk. In common with others who were released from the nightmare of the NKVD interrogation cells he was prone to hallucinations and amnesia, later claiming that his memories had been beaten out of him. He wanted to go to his parents' home in Moscow to recuperate, but he could not remember the address and had to be taken there by friends. After a short period of recovery, Shchegotsky then found himself looking for work. Spartak Moscow, one of the senior teams in the city, offered him an administrative position and an apartment to go with it, but Shchegotsky was determined to play again. He had been captain of Dynamo Kiev before he was imprisoned and when they wrote asking him for talks about rejoining the team, he immediately agreed. Although they had stood by him, a number of the senior Dynamo players were doubtful about whether or not Shchegotsky could be the player he once had been. It was agreed privately that if he felt he was not up to it then he would be free to leave the team without any recrimination on either side. But, remarkably, after a spell in a sanatorium on the Black Sea and a few months of good food and regular exercise, Konstantin Shchegotsky returned to full health. He rejoined the Dynamo first team at the beginning of the 1940 season and although he was in his thirties and one of the oldest in the team, he provided the experience and craft which was required in a team which was showing signs of becoming stale and losing its pre-eminence. He also re-formed the potent striking partnership with Nikolai Makhinya. Many were surprised to see two supposed ideological opponents working so effectively together. In one final Machiavellian move, the NKVD spread an elaborate rumour to cover Shchegotsky's disappearance for almost two seasons. They let it be known that he had been having a passionate affair with the wife of the Swedish consul in Moscow and was so in love with her that he had run off to Scandinavia to be with her. Now that she had broken his heart, he had returned. Because he and his team-mates were sworn to secrecy about the truth and because the story fitted so well with Shchegotsky's image as a womanising playboy, no one questioned it.

And so in September 1941, Shchegotsky found himself defending Kiev with the same devotion that the Dynamo players had shown in protecting him. But the war would fragment the Dynamo Kiev team – inevitably and irrevocably. Shchegotsky himself had a chance parting amid the chaos of a city in complete collapse.

On the morning of 19 September our unit was retreating and we joined a military column. German planes were bombing the column and had done a lot of damage. When the air raid was over I bumped into Ivan Kuzmenko. His unit was moving very slowly along a highway that was blocked by a lot of military equipment. Ivan suggested we try to fight our way out together, but because there was no more space on his truck, we simply embraced and said goodbye and hoped we would see each other again. But it never happened. Vanya [Kuzmenko] stayed in the encirclement just like Klimenko and Trusevich and Korotkykh and some of the others. I was lucky. After sixty-seven days of wandering I found our troops at Rostov. Burdukov – one of our other players – vanished without trace, we never knew what became of him.

Shchegotsky owed everything to his adopted team and his adopted city. Now he was forced away from both. His city had lost its greatest battle, but for the remnants of his team their greatest contest still lay ahead and Konstantin Shchegotsky, who had shared so many triumphs with his comrades, would not be able to play his part.

# CHAPTER FIVE

The surrender of Kiev was total and comprehensive. The Germans took some 630,000 prisoners when the city fell, which remains the largest number of soldiers taken captive in a single action throughout history. The original complement of the Red Army at the Battle of Kiev had only been 677,000, which provides a graphic illustration of the catastrophic scale of the defeat. The number of prisoners seems accurate, even though after the war the Soviets disputed it. Their final figure of just over half a million is hardly much more encouraging. The large number of prisoners posed enormous problems for the German occupiers, whose initial response was to place them in huge open-air prisoner-of-war camps like the one at Darnitsa on the banks of the Dnieper. Not long after he said his farewells to Shchegotsky, Kolya Trusevich had been taken prisoner and he ended up in Darnitsa. One of the first people he met there was Nikolai Balakin, also a footballer. Balakin had played for Lokomotiv, Kiev's local rivals. The rivalry was confined to the football field, the players from both teams mixed off the pitch and Balakin and Trusevich bonded instantly in the camp.

These camps were not organised like the killing factories of Auschwitz or Bergen-Belsen. They were vast holding compounds where the captured could be detained until they were 'processed' – classified according to their perceived threat. In many ways Darnitsa, and other camps like it throughout the conquered Soviet Union, resembled earlier models from the Anglo-Boer War or the American Civil War. In 1864, for example, the camp at Andersonville in Georgia, which had been custom built to hold 10,000 Union soldiers, was sickeningly overcrowded. There were 32,000 men held there by August of that year. The combined effects of little food, no sanitation and the unhealthy climate took a terrible toll. Disease was rife; scurvy, dysentery, diarrhoea and gangrene raged unchecked. In its fourteen-month existence one in three of the Northern prisoners sent to Andersonville died there. It was a similar story at the turn of the century in South Africa when Lord Kitchener's scorched earth policy, ordered in March 1901, destroyed 30,000 Boer farmhouses and devastated around forty townships. Thousands of people, mostly women and children, were interned in huge concentration camps without adequate food, hygiene or shelter and with no medical supplies or medical staff. Just over 26,000 women and children – 80 per cent of them children – died in these British concentration camps.

Conditions in Darnitsa would be no better than in any of the other prisoner-of-war camps which were springing up across the Soviet Union as the Germans advanced.

There was little shelter beyond some rudimentary barracks, which meant the prisoners, many of them grievously wounded, were exposed to the heat of the day – and the September days were still hot – followed by the bitter cold of the autumn night. Many were unable to cope with the extremes of temperature and died. Sanitary conditions were rudimentary, disease was rife. The biggest killer of all, however, was starvation. The Germans had been encouraged to believe the Bolsheviks were subhuman. They made no distinction between Russian, Ukrainian or Belorussian. They were all simply the hated enemy and as such beneath contempt and scarcely worth the bother of feeding, even though the Germans had more than enough food stockpiled. This was a direct reflection of the views held in Nazi Berlin. As far as the *Übermenschen* – the supermen of the Aryan race – were concerned, the Ukrainians and the Jews were *Untermenschen*, subhumans to be purged so that Hitler's targets could be met. He was so determined to possess the *Lebensraum* of the Ukraine that he effectively sanctioned a campaign of total annihilation against the Ukrainians. Hitler fully expected that within one year of occupying the region, the bulk of the population would either have 'disappeared' or been sent back to Germany as a slave labour force. The Geneva Convention was unheard of on the Eastern Front.

In some camps the German guards taunted the prisoners by throwing food into the compound as though they were throwing stale bread to ducks. The captured Soviets lost all trace of dignity as they clamoured and fought for the smallest scraps. Cannibalism was common practice in many of the camps. Some of the prisoners died knowing at least that they might keep some of their comrades in arms alive for a little longer. Even if they were able to survive all this, there was also the constant threat of being sent to the feared death camp at Siretz. The survival rate at Siretz was very low and the regime was appallingly cruel even by the standards that prevailed elsewhere. Being sent to Siretz was tantamount to a death sentence, the only question being how long it would take to die. Trusevich and Balakin had already survived one raid by the guards, who had come into the barracks at Darnitsa one morning and simply rousted out everyone they could find. Prisoners were told they were going to Siretz, but instead they were simply taken outside and shot. For most it was a more merciful alternative. Trusevich and Balakin had managed to conceal themselves under some bedding at the rear of the barracks. Among so many captured soldiers it was almost impossible for the Germans to say with any accuracy how many prisoners were supposed to be in each hut. By the greatest of good fortune no one came looking for them and Balakin and Trusevich survived. Their former team-mate Yatchmennikov was not so fortunate, he was among the many who perished in Darnitsa.

Conditions in Kiev itself were not much better than in Darnitsa. Everything that could be of any conceivable use to the occupying forces had been blown up or burned. What had not been destroyed by the retreating troops had been pulverised and pounded by the German bombardment. The once beautiful and elegant buildings looked like two-dimensional façades on a movie set. The street fighting had left huge gaps in the rows of buildings where

German Panzers and armoured cars had taken advantage of the broad avenues to simply roll in and pound them with their cannon. The flames which had roared through the windows left the outside walls black with soot, and the constant exchanges of gunfire meant there was scarcely a window left unbroken. But still the resistance of the people of Kiev was not completely broken.

One of the first tasks of the occupying German force in September was to set up a military headquarters in Kreschatik Street, the main street of the city, from which they could impose a new order on the people of Kiev. Very quickly most of the military and civil authorities were established there. Less than a week later, in one final act of defiance, a team of NKVD officers that had remained hidden in the city was able to dynamite half the buildings in the street. The devastation was staggering. With no civilian firemen and no one in the military willing to volunteer, the buildings burned for days. According to eyewitnesses Kreschatik was still burning when the following notice was posted around the city on 27 September, three days after the blast.

On Monday, 29 September 1941, all Jews from the city of Kiev and the surrounding area should report at 0800 to the corner of Melnikovskaya and Dokhturovsky Streets. They should take their documents, money, valuables, as well as warm clothes, underwear, etc.

Those Jews who do not fulfil this order and who are found elsewhere will be shot. Those citizens who go into houses left by Jews and steal their belongings will be shot.

As they had done almost everywhere else in Eastern Europe, thousands of Jews turned up promptly with their belongings. Men, women and children of all ages arrived at Melnikovskaya Street where they were then ordered to divide up into columns. There were 100 people in each column, and more than 300 columns in all. Thirty thousand Jews were marched out of the city and told to go to the Lukyanovskoye cemetery. As they made their doleful way out of the city, they could scarcely have been in any doubt about what was going to happen. *En route* to the cemetery they passed other bodies lying in the street and in the gutter. The corpses were not of soldiers but of civilians executed where they stood on the whim of the invaders. Some were Jewish, some were partisans, many were simply in the wrong place at the wrong time. When the Jewish columns finally arrived at the cemetery they were stripped of all their clothing and their valuables. They were then taken to the ravine at Babi Yar.

The Operational Situation Report USSR Number 101, dated 2 October 1941, informs the chiefs of the Security Police and the Security Services in Berlin that 'Sonderkommando 4a in collaboration with Einsatz-gruppe HQ and two Kommandos of Police Regiment South executed 33,771 Jews in Kiev on 29 and 30 September 1941.'

According to another official report 'the action was carried out without any complications and no incidents happened'. The clothing, the valuables and everything else which had been taken from the Jews were divided out amongst all of those who took part in the Babi Yar shootings. Among the executioners were divisions of

Nazi-sympathising Ukrainian policemen as well as German soldiers.

The first few months in occupied Kiev were a waking nightmare of constant starvation and random brutality for the people of the city. There seemed never enough food to go round. The Germans had huge stockpiles to supply their own troops and it seems likely that there would also have been enough for the civilian population, it was simply that they had no interest in keeping them alive. Very soon the people of Kiev were reduced to eating domestic animals and before long there was not a dog or a cat left in the city. The rats which swarmed in from the Dnieper were also fair game but even they could not provide enough to live on. What little poultry remained had been used up quickly and there was nothing else to replace it. There were very few birds of any kind around after the Germans discovered that pigeons were being used to pass messages between resistance groups. The Germans instantly ordered that all of the pigeons be shot or poisoned. People made soups from grass, leaves, pieces of leather, anything they could find. The Germans meanwhile made life more difficult at every opportunity, they had little compassion for their vanquished enemies. Hitler's plan was simply that the Ukrainians would either remain as slaves or be starved into extinction. Later, in December 1942, he would order that 'the most brutal means' be used against the Ukraine, even to the extent of specifying that women and children should not be exempt from the reprisals.

Although they were living under the most dreadful conditions there was one thing in which the Kievans were united. Whether they were left in the city or whether they endured the lingering torments of Darnitsa and similar institutions, their strong attachment to the Motherland remained undiminished. All that differed was how that bond manifested itself. Fervent Stalinists like Nikolai Makhinya felt ashamed at being taken prisoner and would much rather have died in the defence of the Motherland. But there were others who reflected a growing mood in the Ukraine which held that life under Hitler could not be any less oppressive than life under Stalin. Despite the desperate consequences for many of those who stayed behind, there were those who welcomed the invaders. Contemporary photographs and newsreels show Ukrainian women, dressed in national costume, lining the streets to cheer the Germans as if they were an army of liberation. Some of these pictures and films are surely nothing more than Nazi propaganda exercises staged after the event, but even so they are merely an exaggeration of an evident truth. There were a great many people in the Ukraine who were heartily sick of Stalinism and what it had done to them. These were not people who remembered the 'good old days' of Tsarist rule, these were people whose memories needed only to stretch back fewer than ten years to the Great Hunger. These were the people who made up the crowds who waved and cheered and offered the incoming armies the traditional Ukrainian hospitality of bread and salt.

Among the Dynamo Kiev players one of the prime movers of the view that things would improve under Hitler was Lazar Kogen, who was what would now be termed a squad player. Kogen reasoned, as did many others, that it could not be any worse than under Stalin. In any case, their argument went, where would they escape to? The Germans were everywhere and appeared to be unstoppable. Although Kogen was Jewish he remembered that the Germans had treated the Jews no worse than anyone else during the occupation in the First World War. Kogen, a persuasive speaker, was able to convince many of the players, one by one, to stay in the city. He spoke to Lev Chernobylsky, a referee by 1941, but one of the first managers of Dynamo Kiev. Chernobylsky like Kogen was Jewish, but he was persuaded to stay. Kogen also managed to talk Sviridovsky into staying. Makar Goncharenko also stayed but he really did not require much persuading. Goncharenko was a supremely talented winger and an irrepressible character. Politics were the furthest thing from his mind, he simply believed that even the Germans would want to play football and that was all he cared to believe. Goncharenko had managed to keep his strip and a pair of boots with him all through the fighting because he sincerely felt that whichever regime was in power he would be able to play football.

Lazar Kogen was desperately and tragically wrong and he paid for his mistake. He and Lev Chernobylsky were among the first to be shot in the massacres at Babi Yar. Lokomotiv player Vladimir Balakin was also arrested at the beginning of the occupation. He was more fortunate. It emerged that the German army was looking for his brother Nikolai, who was in the Darnitsa camp with Trusevich. Nikolai was a member of the Communist Party but Vladimir was not. He insisted they had got the wrong man, but the Germans appeared not to care. Vladimir was in a room in the Gestapo headquarters waiting for what he suspected would be a cursory interrogation followed by a savage beating and then most likely an execution. As he was sitting there a local official, who was assisting the German administration of Kiev, stuck his head round the door, saw Vladimir, and burst out laughing. The man had been a ticket-seller at the new Red Army stadium and knew they had taken the wrong brother. Balakin was allowed to leave, making him one of the few prisoners to go into the building and come out alive.

It is hard to believe that the Dynamo players genuinely did not realise the danger they were in. Some of the older team members had been aware of the danger before Kiev fell into the hands of the Germans, but theirs does not appear to have been a widespread opinion. Unlike the ordinary citizens of the newly-occupied city, the members of Dynamo Kiev were nominally policemen and as such they were frequent attendees at Communist gatherings and Party meetings. Some of them were even listed as members of the NKVD in official team documents. Their reason for joining the police or the NKVD may have been to entitle them to play for Dynamo and have access to superior training facilities, but this would not make a Gestapo interrogator sympathetic. They had documents which declared them to be secret policemen and as such they could be singled out for some particularly savage treatment by the occupying forces. The danger was compounded by the presence of informers always willing to identify members of the NKVD – footballers or not – to save their lives or feed their families. Others were motivated simply by revenge.

Oleg Golovchenko had helped to found the Dynamo

handball team in 1928, but he had been jailed in the repressions of the thirties because his training methods had been deemed to be 'bourgeois'. Although he was released after a fairly short spell in prison he bore a grudge against the club, whom he blamed for his incarceration. He helped the Gestapo by identifying and even interrogating suspected communists. A great many sportsmen and women from Dynamo's various sports clubs suffered at his hands. In the face of mass executions and people like Oleg Golovchenko helping the Germans, the remaining Dynamo Kiev footballers were taking enormous risks.

# CHAPTER SIX

After the experience of a decade that would for ever be remembered for the Great Hunger and the Terror it is hardly surprising that some Ukrainians regarded the Germans as a force, if not for good, then one that would end Stalinist oppression. The Organisation of Ukrainian Nationalists was an anti-communist, pro-independence terrorist group working in Poland with funding from Germany and Lithuania. Seeing a force which could be manipulated to their own ends the Nazis encouraged the OUN so much that, when German troops invaded in June 1941, they were joined by two OUN units which were under the command of German intelligence.

Large areas of the Ukraine, especially in the West, had never really felt themselves part of communist Russia and many Ukrainians genuinely hoped that Hitler would allow the establishment of a separate Ukraine. Nationalist feelings ran high in the region and the population was sharply divided between those who tolerated communism and Stalin and those who favoured separatism. At first the Germans gave the appearance of supporting the nationalists, which made life considerably easier in the early days of the occupation. The Ukrainian flag was allowed to fly over Kiev and on official buildings under the new regime it was displayed alongside the Swastika. Encouraged by what they saw as an air of tolerance from their new masters, many of the residents of Kiev cooperated to the extent that the Germans found no shortage of recruits to their new paramilitary police force. Even the massacres of the Jews within a week of the city falling did not dispel the belief that for many people life would be better, or at least no worse, under the Germans.

Another Operational Situation Report – this time Number 112, dated 13 October 1941 – suggested that when it came to the twin problems of Bolshevism and Judaism, the people of Kiev were of one mind with their new masters.

The population rejects Bolshevism almost without exception, since there is practically no family which has not lost one or more members through Bolshevik deportation or killing. Also, the Ukrainians had been free farmers and independent in ancient Russia and have not forgotten that everything was taken from them when they were forced into the collective farms. The number of Ukrainians who joined the Communist Party out of conviction is surprisingly low.

The report suggested that only the young, who knew little of life before communism, were convinced by the Party ideology. Even then it suggested that their conviction was not so firm that it could not be swayed by German propaganda to the point where the population could be almost totally re-educated.

> The Ukrainian rejects Judaism together with communism, as it was mainly Jews who were officials of the Communist Party. The Ukrainians had the opportunity to discover that practically only the Jews enjoyed the advantages connected with the membership of the Communist Party, especially in its leading positions . . . There are no leading personalities and no spiritual impetus with the Ukrainian population to trigger off persecution since all remember the harsh punishments inflicted by the Bolsheviks against anyone who attacked the Jews . . . However, if an impulse comes from any side and should the population be given a free hand, an extensive persecution of the Jews could result.

The OUN's charismatic young leader Stepan Bandera had all but declared war on the Jews as recently as 1939 when he was released from prison in Poland by the Germans. Bandera was the leader of the militant wing of the OUN and had been imprisoned for terrorist offences. The OUN modelled itself along Fascist lines. Anyone who joined had to swear a series of ten oaths, the first of which pledged them to 'attain a Ukrainian state or die in battle for it'. There is little doubt that Bandera's feelings were reflected in the nationalist community as a whole, who believed, as he did, that the Jews were the staunchest supporters of the Bolsheviks. It is surprising, therefore, that the Kiev players decided to stay in the city however persuasive Lazar Kogen's assurances that they would be well treated had been. For example, Livshitz, his sister and niece, who were Trusevich's wife and daughter, were Jewish, ethnically if not through practice. This feeling of anti-Jewishness was ruthlessly exploited by the Germans. The executions at Babi Yar became weekly occurrences, yet generated scarcely a word of protest from the Ukrainian inhabitants of Kiev. Indeed, when the belongings of those who had been executed were sold in the market, the Ukrainians queued as enthusiastically as the Germans to buy their possessions.

But soon it became apparent that the executions were not merely confined to the Jews. The OUN misread the political situation when it proclaimed a 'Sovereign All-Ukrainian State' and became caught in the middle of a bitter power struggle for control of the Ukraine. The nominal head of the Ostministerium – the ministry responsible for administering German rule in the east – was Alfred Rosenberg. He was a political philosopher who had been loyal to Hitler before he came to power and had been rewarded for his loyalty by admission to Hitler's inner circle. He had been the head of the foreign political section in the National Socialist Party office and was appointed Minister of the Eastern Territories in April 1941. Rosenberg was very pro-Ukrainian, and had a plan to establish a separate Ukrainian state by taking territory away from Russia. He even wanted to establish a University of the Ukraine. Rosenberg's notion was that a separatist Ukraine would act as a sort of buffer state between the Reich and any future threat from the east. Hitler gave him the impression that he agreed and Rosenberg was convinced that an autonomous Ukraine could exist within the new German empire. Rosenberg's biggest problem seems to have been an inability to distinguish the abstract from the concrete. He was an occasionally insightful political theorist but had very little grasp of realpolitik. Although it was obvious to everyone else but Rosenberg, Hitler had no intention of allowing any autonomous Ukrainian state to survive. The Ukraine must be crushed. Rosenberg was allowed to indulge himself with grand visions, but on the very day that Kiev fell, 19 September 1941, minutes of a meeting between Hitler and Erich Koch, the newly-created Reichs-kommissar – the actual administrator in the Ukraine – show Hitler's genuine feelings. Hitler told Koch he absolutely rejected the notion of a new Ukrainian state. In addition he felt that all the major cities would have to be razed to the ground and the industrial infrastructure would have to be smashed so that the Ukrainians would effectively be forced back into serfdom. Koch was close to Hitler and had known him since 1922. He was a protégé of Goering who had advanced his cause whenever the opportunity arose. Through Goering, Koch also had the support of Himmler and Martin Bormann. Rosenberg, by contrast, had no close allies within the ranks of those competing for the Führer's favour and was a very poor politician. He was not well regarded by Hitler's most trusted policy advisers, but the historian Alan Clark suggests that, although he was not a particularly bright minister, Rosenberg suited Hitler's purposes. Fearing, as the Caesars had once done, a potential revolt from the provinces Hitler would rather have had a dull but biddable Ostminister than a sharp and ambitious one. Although Koch as Minister for the

Ukraine was required to report to Rosenberg, his superior as Minister for the East, the two men clashed frequently. Rosenberg did wring a concession from Hitler that the Führer would only see Koch when the Ostminister was present. This may have satisfied Rosenberg, but in reality the concession was meaningless since the Reichskommissar for the Ukraine had access to Hitler through Goering or Bormann. It was Koch who really had Hitler's ear, and it would be Koch's vision, shared with his Führer, that would prevail.

Erich Koch, a former railway official, was an extraordinarily cruel man who set about Hitler's wishes with a will. He and Goering were of the opinion that the only way to deal with the Ukraine was through ethnic cleansing. They advocated killing all the men over fifteen and sending in 'the SS stallions'. In his inauguration speech he revelled in his own description of himself as 'a brutal dog'. Koch went on to tell the assembled troops that their job was to suck from the Ukraine everything they could get hold of, and he expected them to treat the local population with the utmost severity. He genuinely believed that the Ukrainians were subhuman and would not allow his troops to waste ammunition on them. His favoured punishment was whipping, sometimes to death. In November 1941 he ordered twenty Ukrainians to be whipped because it was alleged they had sabotaged a bridge being built across the Dnieper. Alan Clark describes scenes of 'pre-Roman barbarism' under 'the sadistic Koch'. Gangs of so-called volunteers were driven under the lash to railway trucks which would take them to slave labour in Germany and almost certain death. It was a daily occurrence.

It was under Erich Koch that the practice of ordering the deaths of 100 Ukrainians for every German soldier shot by partisans was introduced. Other Koch deterrents included public hangings after which the bodies were left to rot for several days as a warning to the rest of the populace. Discipline under Koch was arbitrary but unfailingly brutal. Peasants could be shot as intellectuals for admitting they could read and write. Pregnant women were forced to have abortions as he attempted to wipe out the Ukrainian race. A Kievan could be flogged for failing to take off his cap to a German officer. Anyone deemed to be holding back food in the collective farms which the Nazis had reorganised as 'cooperatives', could be hanged. Historians suggest that as many as 250 Ukrainian villages were wiped from the map to encourage the remainder to comply with German rule.

Koch's views on education were similarly extreme. Hitler had once told him that Ukrainians should only be given the crudest kind of education so that they could communicate effectively with their German masters. Koch immediately ordered the schools and colleges to be closed to anyone over the age of fifteen and all of the students and teachers to be sent to Germany as slave labour. Only the first four grades were to be taught at school; even Hitler agreed that minimal literacy and numeracy was useful and practical. The universities were shut down.

Given Koch's closeness to Hitler, it was a huge strategic misjudgement for the OUN and Stepan Bandera to announce the setting up of a new independent government of the Ukraine. This administration, with Yaroslav Stetsko as its Prime Minister, was effectively a government in exile biding its time but fully expecting to be in power in the Ukraine in a short while. This was simply too much for the Germans and even the normally mild-mannered Rosenberg would not have been able to tolerate the presumption. A week after the new administration was announced it was disbanded and its members arrested. Bandera and Stetsko spent the war in Sachsenhausen Prison in Germany.

As Koch's new regime took hold in Kiev informers had all but made sure that large-scale partisan and resistance operations were brought under control. But like the bombing of the Kreschatik there continued to be sporadic acts of isolated sabotage and civil disobedience. In November 1941, in one of the most spectacular incidents, the cathedral in the Pecherska Lavra monastery was blown up. The monastery which was a much loved local landmark had been built in 1073, not long after the Great Golden Gate which was itself by this stage a crumbling ruin. The Moscow propagandists tried to blame the destruction on the Germans, but it appears to have been the work of a Ukrainian booby trap squad. They had mined it before they left, like the Kreschatik, and then detonated the explosives when the monastery was full of German troops.

Acts of sabotage drew reprisals of summary brutality and the results were posted in the streets so that no one could be mistaken about the consequences of such actions. The mass execution at Babi Yar on 29 and 30 September was merely the beginning. A notice was posted in the city on 27 October, for example, announcing that 'as a reprisal for an act of sabotage 100 inhabitants of Kiev were shot'.

A few days later on 2 November, the day before the monastery bombing, another poster appeared.

I am forced to undertake the strictest possible measures because of more and more frequent cases of arson and sabotage. For this reason today 300 inhabitants of Kiev were shot. For each new case of arson or sabotage many more inhabitants will be shot. Each inhabitant of Kiev is obliged to inform the German police about each suspicious incident. I will ensure order and calm in Kiev by any and all measures and in all circumstances.

The Germans were as good as their word. On 29 November another poster appeared.

In Kiev, telephones, telegraphs, cables and other means of communication have been deliberately damaged. Because it is impossible to tolerate these wreckers any more, 400 men have been shot in the city, which should serve as a warning to the population. I demand once again that all suspicious incidents should be immediately reported to the German troops or the German police so that the criminals can be duly punished.

All of these orders were signed by Major-General Eberhardt, then the military commander of the city, acting under the instructions of Erich Koch.

One of the worst incidents came at the Poltava lunatic asylum in Kiev. The Germans required the building and its grounds for use as a field hospital and acquired them with a staggering savagery. A fleet of German trucks and vans arrived at Poltava between 31 October and 5 November. All week long inmates were bundled into the vehicles and taken away to be exterminated. After the war one of the hospital doctors provided a horrific testimony to the Soviet War Crimes Tribunal.

He told how a group of SS officers arrived on 14 October. They were advised by doctors from the local garrison and they selected around 300 patients. These unfortunates were then put into one of the hospital out-buildings and left for several days with neither food nor water. After that, according to the doctor, a convoy of vans came to the hospital. The Germans started pushing people into the vans, sixty or seventy people in each van, then they took them to a ravine in the Kirilov woods. In the woods, the patients were shot and their bodies thrown into a gully. The killings were not always so clean. Some patients were tortured. Some, already sick and weak, were beaten senseless and then shot. The killings went on for several days and by the end of the ordeal more than 800 patients and inmates had been murdered.

The official Operational Report from Einsatzgruppe C says that 599 'mentally ill persons' were killed at Poltava during this week. It says that a further 200 inmates were sent to work in a nearby agricultural plant. These 200 souls would almost certainly have died within days or weeks under slave labour conditions. This would account for the 800 patients in the doctor's testimony. Poltava was turned over to the Wehrmacht as a field hospital and all of the 'underwear, clothing and household articles' were placed at its disposal.

Any notions the Kievans may have had about a better

life under the German invaders had by now been quickly and brutally dispelled. The Ukrainian flag no longer flew above Kiev and Nazism was the only political philosophy allowed to prevail. By the end of November around 100,000 civilians had been executed – including 75,000 Jews – and the people of Kiev could be in no doubt that they had merely exchanged the insidious terror of Stalin for the instant reprisal of the Einsatzgruppen.

But the occupying German army needed Kiev to function. It was an important staging post for supplying the ongoing advance. Having subdued the rebellious elements, Kiev had to be allowed to discover its new role under German administration and essential elements of urban life were restored. The Germans issued a new currency – the *karbowanetz* – which, with perverse irony, featured pictures of idealised Ukrainian peasants on the front of the notes. Then, one of their first jobs was to classify and stratify the population, which they did along the same lines applied in other occupied territories. The new Kiev would operate under a four-tier caste system designed purely and simply on racial terms.

At the top of the social strata were the Reichsdeutsche who were Germans who had been living in Germany. These pure-bred Aryans, whether they were soldiers or administrators, could largely do what they pleased and lorded it over the local population. If the Reichsdeutsche were the new aristocracy, then one tier below them came the Volksdeutsche. Strictly speaking these were Germans who were living outside Germany or living in German colonies. In practice, in the occupied territories the definition could be stretched to those who could prove some sort of reasonable German provenance.

Although not in the supreme position of the Reichsdeutsche, those who were categorised as Volksdeutsche did have a great many advantages. They could, for example, run businesses and they were given preferential treatment in terms of employment, accommodation and every other aspect of daily living. The Volksdeutsche also comprised the bulk of the new bureaucratic hierarchy in Kiev. Although they were deemed inferior to the Reichsdeutsche, the Volksdeutsche were conspicuously superior to the rest of the population and enjoyed a more than tolerable standard of living, with access to money, food and travel.

Although the Germans put into place a social system with a clearly defined upper and middle tier, it would be a mistake to think of the third category as a conventional working class. The vanquished local population constituted a large group of people whose continued existence depended largely on the whim of the first two categories. They had no automatic rights whatsover. They were treated as human fodder to be worked until they dropped and then cast aside on the scrap heap of a mass grave. Finally, in the lowest category of all were those who were deemed to be enemies of the Reich. These were Communist Party members, local officials and others considered dangerous. Those who had not been immediately shot or thrown into a concentration camp were kept under constant surveillance. They had regularly to register at special offices. This fourth category also contained those who had fought against the Reich but were not necessarily deemed to pose a serious threat now that the war, as far as the Germans were concerned, had been won.

Members of this grouping included captured Soviet enlisted men rather than officers, those who had not been Party members, and those who had not held any kind of government office under the communists. The German argument ran that it was a waste of time keeping these men in the prisoner-of-war camps, they would be much more useful in the workforce. So it was decided that if they were willing to sign a declaration promising to be loyal to the new regime, they would be allowed out of the camps. All of those Dynamo Kiev players captured in the encirclement signed the papers. There was little option for Trusevich, Kuzmenko, Klimenko and the others. Many of them, simply by virtue of playing for Dynamo, could be considered members of the Communist Party. In fact, most of these players would not have considered themselves to be active communists or Party members, they were simply footballers who would have joined any organisation if it had meant they would get a game. They were not politicians, they were pragmatists. They also must have realised that failure to sign these declarations would have meant that they were effectively condemning themselves to death, whether in a camp or in a prison cell or from a bullet. And there were their families to be considered. If they did not sign the papers then the Germans would have no hesitation in declaring their families to be enemies of the Reich and that would mean, at best, imprisonment for the relatives and loved ones. In the end Trusevich, Klimenko, Kuzmenko and even the passionate Stalinist Nikolai Makhinya signed the papers and were freed from the detention camps. Other Dynamo players who had also been rounded up in the encirclement – Pavel

Komarov, Makar Goncharenko, Fyodor Tyutchev, Mikhail Sviridovsky and Mikhail Putistin – joined them and were allowed out.

Restoring the industrial infrastructure was another of the main priorities for the German invaders. The further into the Soviet Union the army pushed, the longer were their lines of communication and the more important it was to provide at least a measure of self-sufficiency. One of the first tasks was to get the bakeries working again so that they could provide food, first for the advancing armies and German administrators and then with whatever was left over for the local population. The first to restart work after the occupation was Bakery no. 3 in Degtyarevskaya Street. There is some confusion over the naming of this building. Although before the war it had been known as no. 3, the Germans referred to it as 'Bakery no. 1' because it had the most modern machinery and was the first to reopen. After the war it reverted to its original name. Bakery no. 3, as its industrially pragmatic name implied, was not a bakery in the sense that we perhaps imagine them in small English towns or in Parisian *arrondissements*. It was a major industrial complex – in Ukrainian it is known as 'Khlebzavod' which means bread plant – and, from the outside, looked no different from any other big factory in Kiev. The sole function of Bakery no. 3 was to make bread in sufficient quantity to address the demands of thousands of people every day and it was capable of producing more than 50 tonnes of different types of bread on a daily basis. It was not a cottage industry, less still a hand-crafted procedure, but a well-ordered manufacturing process and it took the combined skills of up to 300 people to achieve the end result. Before the war the bakery had been run by Alexander Levkovich who was a skilled engineer with many years' experience. However, when it was reopened Levkovich was merely the deputy and Iosif Ivanovich Kordik was the new boss. Kordik's elevation was a clear example of the new reclassification in the Ukraine where advancement was a consequence of bloodline rather than ability.

Almost immediately after the occupation of Kiev, Iosif Kordik had made a small but significant change in his name. He went from being Iosif Ivanovich to Iosif Jorganovich, taking a Teutonic equivalent of his patronymic. This was one of a number of small measures which Kordik took to prove to the new masters that he was and would continue to be a good and loyal servant of the Reich. To begin with it seemed that Kordik's 'conversion' was designed for personal advancement, although as the occupation wore on and his dis-satisfaction with the German rulers increased, other, possibly more altruistic, reasons would emerge. Life had not been easy and Kordik had borne a number of grudges against the Ukrainians for many years. Events in 1941 seemed to provide him with a chance to tip the scales back in his direction. To begin with Kordik was not German, he was in fact a Moravian Czech who had been born at the end of the nineteenth century in land which was then part of the Austro-Hungarian empire. As a young man he fought in the First World War for the Hapsburgs. He was wounded and ended up in Kiev, where he had lived ever since. Although his wounds quickly healed Kordik never tried to return to Moravia. At first he was not allowed to, but later he seemed to nurse his bitterness considering himself trapped in his new country. Some of Kordik's frustration was perhaps understandable. He had been wounded, he was – in his own opinion at least – being held against his will, and it seemed whatever chance he had for happiness had been snatched away from him. Not long after the First World War he had met and fallen in love with a local girl, which may have had something to do with his lack of desire to go home even when he was finally able. They were married, but she died not long afterwards leaving Kordik to bring up a baby daughter on his own. It was probably his devotion to the little girl and his unwillingness to take her into an uncertain future in Moravia which, more than anything, contributed to Kordik's sense that he had become stranded in a foreign land.

Iosif Kordik spoke German like a native. Seizing his opportunity in 1941, he lied about his birthplace and told the new authorities that he came from Austria. With his fluent German and his eagerness to please, the Germans were not inclined to investigate his case too closely and he was duly categorised as one of the Volksdeutsche. He returned to work in the bakery, where he had worked before the war, but now he was in charge since Alexander Levkovich had been recategorised as a third-class citizen. Levkovich does not appear to have resented either the Germans or Kordik for his reversal. He said some years later that Kordik did not really hate the Soviet authorities, even though they had prevented him from going home. All he really wanted, according to Levkovich, was to feel as though he was living a full and useful life and might one day finally find some kind of freedom in his original home, Moravia.

His feelings of gloom and resentment hung around Kordik like a shroud. He was a small, humourless man who worked long hours without a break and seemed to have no life beyond the bakery. Many who worked with him did not even know that he had a daughter, small talk was not his forte. As well as being something of a sharp dresser, Kordik was also rather fat and with his scrubbed, pink features he looked, according to one former employee, Anna Varshavskaya, like a freshly baked bun. Varshavskaya also offers another insight into Kordik's personality. She described him as being reserved and taciturn at work but with the potential to be very severe and extraordinarily cruel. Certainly there is evidence to back this up as the German occupation of Kiev wore on. There was one subject, however, that could be guaranteed to bring Kordik to life. He was passionate about sport, especially football, and was a fanatical Dynamo Kiev fan. The only time anyone remembers this small, sad man become animated and voluble was in connection with sport.

Towards the end of 1941, Kordik was out walking in Kiev when he stopped for a bite to eat. As he was sitting at a café in Mikhailovskaya Street – naturally the café was also now owned by a member of the Volksdeutsche – he saw someone whom he thought he recognised. At first he was not sure, but eventually he was convinced that the man he was looking at was Nikolai Trusevich. It is hardly surprising that Kordik did not recognise the man he had vigorously cheered when he was in goal for Kiev. His own team-mate Shchegotsky had barely recognised him and since then he had endured a couple of months in Darnitsa which had further transformed this tall, elegant, debonair man. He was thin and gaunt. A combination of exhaustion and his leg injury left him walking with a limp. What remained of his army greatcoat hung off him in rags and the man who had been so fastidious about his appearance had not been able to wash or shave properly in weeks. The only thing that convinced Kordik that he was indeed looking at the great Kolya Trusevich was the signature scar on his right cheek. Kordik was horrified that the great Trusevich had been reduced to this. He bought him something to eat and the two men talked.

Kordik quickly learned that Trusevich, like so many others, had been living a hand-to-mouth existence. He had been allowed out of the camp at Darnitsa, but with limits on where he could go and with no official place to stay life had been almost impossible. He had worked where and when he could – a day here, a day there – and eaten whenever he was able. But the prospects were not good. If he did not starve or freeze to death then he would inevitably be picked up either by the Germans or the local police. This would mean either being shipped off to Germany to die as a slave in a factory, or thrown into prison in Kiev and probably either shot or beaten to death. Trusevich, like so many others, was simply a man living under a death sentence which would be carried out at a date yet to be decided. His position was far from unique. Life for the ordinary Kievans was almost un-bearable in the first months of German occupation. Families had been torn apart. Breadwinners were dead, mothers had lost children, children wandered the city looking for parents. Those who had not been killed in the savagery of the conflict fell victim to starvation or to the harsh regime of their new masters. News of friends and loved ones filtered in and out of the city.

That summer, in the early days of the war in the east when no one really believed that the fighting would come to Kiev, the locals had gone about their usual preparations for winter. Fruits were preserved, jams and chutneys were put up, fish was salted. Now that winter had arrived the stocks which had been laid in were either destroyed in the fighting or left mouldering in the rubble with their owners dead and gone. Buying food was theoretically possible but in practice it required something of a miracle. The Reichsdeutsche and the Volksdeutsche never went hungry and they had enough money to pay for what little supplies were available. For the locals it was an entirely different story. Those lucky enough to find work could, if they were extremely fortunate, make somewhere between fifty and 100 roubles a month. If you could find a loaf of wheat bread at the market you could expect to pay forty roubles, a litre of milk would cost twenty roubles, and a pound of potatoes – one of the staples of the Ukrainian diet – could cost anything up to 100 roubles. Butter was almost non-existent in general supply, but if you could find any a kilo could not be had for anything less than 300 roubles. In addition to these basics *salo*, the most common dish in the Ukraine, could cost 340 roubles a pound. *Salo* is basically salted pig fat with a seasoning, such as garlic or pepper. To anyone outside the Soviet Union it is very definitely an acquired taste but for the Ukrainians it is their national staple. It is served with almost every meal and eaten on its own – like tapas in Spain – as a side order with a *ryumka* of vodka. At these prices and with even poorly paid work almost impossible to find, the general population was slowly starving. This, of course, was Koch's policy.

Like everyone else, Trusevich seemed to be resigned to his fate in the short term. There was always the unspoken hope that Stalin and the Red Army would save them in the end, but the immediate prospect was a day-to-day endurance test. He did at least have the satisfaction of knowing that his Jewish wife and daughter were relatively safe for the time being in Odessa. Having seen what had happened to the Jews in Kiev, Trusevich was relieved they had both left. Kordik was appalled by his story and decided to do something to help. He immediately offered Trusevich a full-time job at the bakery. A master baker for almost twenty years, Trusevich was delighted by Kordik's offer and took it up immediately. His new classification, however, prevented him from returning to his former trade no matter how able he was. Although with grain of any kind in such short supply, he would have had trouble recognising the coarse, plain fare being churned out of the bakery, compared to the rich variety of breads he had been used to. Trusevich ended up sweeping the yard and sleeping in one of the dormitories at night. When he started his job at Bakery no. 3, Trusevich was surprised to find that he was not alone.

Iosif Kordik seems to have been a man torn between his love for sport and his desire to do well enough to be allowed to go home. Publicly he supported the Germans. He ran an efficient operation at the bakery and would not tolerate any breach of the rules. Privately, however, he appears to have had his doubts. He felt disappointed at the way the nationalist movement was effectively being strung along, he was also horrified at the reprisals and the wanton executions. His objection seems to have been practical rather than moral, for he simply believed that people would not work well if they were living under the constant threat of random execution. He felt that working the bakery and all the other factories twenty-four hours a day was not good for morale or productivity. The workers had no time to rest, nothing to do outside working hours, and barely enough food to keep them going while they were there. Kordik was certain they needed something else and he also felt, naturally, that sport provided the answer.

Taking Trusevich off the streets had not been an isolated action. When the goalkeeper came to the bakery in Degtyarevskaya Street he found he was not the only sportsman there. There were gymnasts, cyclists, boxers, athletes and many other sporting personalities hidden among the workforce. It would be easy to think of Iosif Kordik as an Oskar Schindler figure hiding these sportsmen and women away from the scrutiny of the Germans. In reality his motives seem to have been a good deal less altruistic. Kordik was a sports fan and like most enthusiasts the idea of spending time with his heroes moved him more than anything else. It seems he simply wanted to have people like Trusevich and others around him, almost like pets, because they made him feel good about himself. They were not given special treatment, indeed like Trusevich they were generally given the most menial jobs. Kordik just wanted them around.

But the arrival of Kolya Trusevich at the bakery seems to have been the catalyst for an idea which had been turning over in Kordik's mind for some time. It stemmed from his conviction that the workers would benefit from something in their lives other than work, something

110

which would take their minds off their numbing daily existence. What they needed, Kordik believed, was a football team.

The dream of a football team could be realised only with the support of a respected and influential player. Kordik alone could not create a team. So, he took the notion to Trusevich whose initial reaction was one of disbelief, hardly surprising given the circumstances. But Kordik was insistent and won him over. There was some logic to the argument. Working at the bakery would provide shelter – since housing was in short supply part of the factory had been converted into makeshift dormitories – as well as a limited amount of food and some measure of security. At one point Trusevich, who despite his lack of formal education was an intelligent man, actually began to find the idea amusing. It was perhaps Czech engineers who had first brought the game to Kiev at the turn of the century after those fairs in Lviv, now here was another Czech doing his best to save the cream of Ukrainian football. Trusevich gave the matter some thought and finally agreed to act as go-between for Kordik. Once he had agreed he had to find those surviving team-mates in Kiev who were by now scattered throughout the city living in the same straitened circumstances as he had until so recently. He spent the spring of 1942 searching the city, trying to put a team together. The first person he called on was Makar Goncharenko who, amid all the chaos and privations, had kept his kit and boots with him because he was convinced that whoever was in charge would want football to be played sooner or later. The little winger was only too delighted to be proved right.

'Kolya came to me at Kreschatik Street where I was living illegally at my former mother-in-law's house,' Goncharenko recalled in a later interview. 'He came to me to have a chat about this idea and to find some of the other boys. We got in touch with Kuzmenko and Sviridovsky and they contacted some of the others.'

Eventually, through a network of contacts, Trusevich was able to reach all the Kiev players who were still in the city. There were not too many. Some, like Shchegotsky, had been fortunate enough to break out of the encirclement and were fighting somewhere else in the war. Others like the goalkeeper Yatchmennikov had perished in the camps. There were those like Lazar Kogen who had been executed by the Germans, and those like Burdukov who had simply disappeared without trace. But Trusevich found those players that he could. He was also persuaded, it seems by Goncharenko as much as anyone else, that he should try to save as many players from other teams as he could. This was no time for internecine rivalry.

'After we had got our own players we also got in touch with some of the boys from Lokomotiv,' Goncharenko remembered. 'We found Mikhail Melnik, Vasily Sukharev and Vladimir Balakin and persuaded them to join us.'

The Lokomotiv players did not require much persuasion. Like for their counterparts from Dynamo, daily existence was a struggle. They needed somewhere to live, they needed food, they needed relative security. So they accepted the proposal.

Iosif Kordik was delighted as more and more famous names were added to his maintenance squad. It was not long before the bakery had a whole courtyard crew of former football players. They spent their days sweeping the yard, loading and unloading. They carried sacks of flour off and trays of bread on to the distribution trucks and reflected on the fact that they now had a chance of seeing out the war. Food was still short but their sporting status benefited them. They had been brought to the bakery by Kordik because they were famous and the other workers at the plant were equally aware of that. Many of the other workers at Bakery no. 3 were just as taken by the idea of having sporting celebrities in the factory as Kordik. The men of Dynamo and Lokomotiv were heroes and their adoring public would do what they could by smuggling food to them whenever it was possible.

'They would throw pieces of bread out of the window down to us in the courtyard,' said Goncharenko. 'We did not have to stay in the courtyard, we were allowed to go into the production areas where they actually baked the bread but we were afraid because there were too many temptations there so we did not go. Anyone who tried to take out any bread would be shot on the spot. So we did not steal, except for little bits.'

This account reveals the other side of Iosif Kordik. Although he may have felt that the German's iron fist tactics were wrong, he was not about to do anything so foolish as complain. When the Germans demanded punishments or reprisals he complied and handed over the workers without a murmur. Goncharenko remembered one particularly chilling incident which brought home to them all the fact that, although they were now safer than they had been on the streets, it was still something of a relative concept.

There was a real danger if anything got broken because the Germans would decide it was sabotage. They would not make any attempt to find out who was right or who was wrong, they would simply put everyone against the wall. Once, I remember, someone threw broken glass into some dough and spoiled the whole batch of bread. The Germans did not even try to find out who did it. They shot the whole crew. There were about twenty-two of them, mostly women and young girls, but they shot them all.

# CHAPTER SEVEN

By the spring of 1942 the Germans had been in control of Kiev for a little more than six months. The preceding winter had again been severe and hundreds of thousands throughout the Ukraine had died of disease, starvation and numbing cold as the temperature dropped to minus 30 celsius. This time the effects were also being felt by the Nazis. 'General Winter' had halted Operation Typhoon, the drive towards Moscow, a mere twenty kilometres from the capital. Walter Schaefer-Kenert was with a Panzer unit at Moscow and recalls how they had to be roused every two hours during the night in case they froze to death in the insidious cold. There were also huge numbers of wounded because men lost fingers and toes to frostbite.

In Kiev and the rest of the Ukraine, hunger continued to be the greatest scourge. Well-fed members of the Wehrmacht stood and watched as people starved to death in front of them. Dignity was cast aside in the desperate search for something to eat. People drank the discarded dishwater which had been used to wash German plates and pots in the hope of finding sustenance from whatever tiny scraps might have remained. Others made soups from grass or from the bark of trees and there were some cases where people simply chewed the bark straight from the birches and chestnuts. The hunger, in particular, played a large part in suffocating the wilfulness of the local population, which allowed the Germans to think that they had, by their own standards, pacified the Kievans. Jews were being relentlessly exterminated, Ukrainians methodically deported to Germany as slave labour, and all without a hitch. It seemed that it would only be a matter of time before Hitler's stated aim of emptying the Ukraine would be achieved. The sabotage and the resistance efforts had largely been put down, although the vicious reprisal executions were continuing. Five people, for example, had to be shot on 4 March 'for abusing the trust of German military forces in the area of distribution of food and clothes to the local population'. But it seemed that the people of Kiev were now largely prepared to live under the German yoke.

This, though, is history seen from a German perspective. For the bulk of the people in Kiev life had been utterly wretched since September 1941 and continued to be so. They had lost all of their freedoms, thanks to the German registration process. This census was a brutally effective means of control. Since everyone had to register, the Germans were able to root out many of the former communist leaders and execute them. Those who chose to avoid the process could also be shot because they did not have the documents they required. Documents could be obtained only by registration. This was such a fail-safe system that the Germans used it as an instrument to weed out certain sectors of the community. They would simply not allow these people to register, so that later they would then be able to execute them on 'legal' grounds for not having the required papers. Basic freedom of movement had also been denied. The people of Kiev lived under a curfew: anyone found on the streets between six at night and five in the morning faced accusations of being a partisan or a criminal and could be shot. They could not leave the city to visit friends or relatives in outlying areas. What movement there was extended only within the city itself. Only those who had been in Kiev on or after 20 September were allowed to stay. Anyone else had been forced out unless they had had good reason for staying, in which case they had had to seek specific permission from the authorities. To reinforce this order, another regulation was issued to the effect that anyone offering shelter or accommodation to anyone who was in the city illegally would be shot along with the person they were sheltering.

In January 1942, a campaign of forced labour had begun. The deportations were announced in the newspaper *Nova Ukrainski Slovo – New Ukrainian Word* – which had replaced the former *Ukrainian Word* newspaper. The original newspaper was very pro-nationalist and was outspoken in its support of Ukrainian independence. Like the OUN, it badly misjudged the mood of the German High Command and the editor Ivan Rohach and his entire staff were taken to Babi Yar and shot. The replacement newspaper was still run by the nationalists but this time under German control and, not surprisingly, took a much more moderate stance on independence. It was as much a mouthpiece for the Fascists as *Pravda* had been for the communists. Whatever appeared in *Nova Ukrainski Slovo* was the version of events approved by the occupying administration.

On 11 January 1942, *Nova Ukrainski Slovo* announced:

Ukrainian men and women, Bolshevik commissars have destroyed your factories and your work places and deprived you of earnings and bread. Germany gives you the chance of useful and well-paid work.

During the journey you will be given good supplies and you will have hot food. In Germany you will be well provided for and find good living conditions. Your wages will be good and you will be paid at the going rate according to your productivity. All the time you are away working in Germany your families will be looked after.

Men and women of all professions – preferably steelworkers between the ages of seventeen and fifty – who would like to volunteer to go to Germany should come to the employment centre in Kiev daily between 0800 and 1500.

The first train was due to leave on 28 January. The relentlessly upbeat tone of the newspaper announcement made the offer sound unfeasibly attractive. Many doubtless suspected as much but there were enough people seduced by the spurious promise of regular food and safe accommodation. The places on the train were filled by 22 January. Another newspaper advertisement appeared in March with a similarly bullish exhortation.

'Germany calls you! Go to Beautiful Germany!' said this announcement. '100,000 Ukrainians are already working in free Germany. What about you?'

This met with considerably less success than the first notice. No matter how much encouragement the paper offered, word had filtered back to the Ukraine about the conditions facing these so-called Ostarbeiter – 'eastern workers'. Every word of the original newspaper announcement had been a lie. The luckless volunteers found themselves packed into cattle trucks on their journey, they were fed little more than starvation rations before being housed in labour camps. Those who did not succumb to hunger or exhaustion or were not shot at the whim of their new 'employers' for any infraction of the rules, survived only to die later in Allied air raids on Germany. Estimates suggest around 2.2 million of the Ostarbeiter came from the Ukraine. There are no reliable figures for the small proportion who returned to the Soviet Union.

Even so, Germany needed workers whether they were willing or not. Hitler had ordered Erich Koch to provide 450,000 workers a year from the Ukraine. The German response to the lack of volunteers was simply to make the operation mandatory. On 21 March, Hitler passed an order making it compulsory for all childless women between the ages of sixteen and forty-five, or those women whose children were older than sixteen to be registered so they could be sent to work in Germany. Once these orders were in place some 40,000 Ukrainians were sent every month. Yet Hitler's Armaments Minister and logistical overseer Albert Speer constantly complained that the workforce was dwindling. Simple arithmetic suggests the horrifying reality that more than 40,000 men, women and children were dying every month in Germany, either in transit, or working as slaves, or later as victims of Allied bombing raids.

That the Ostarbeiters had to be pressed into the trucks destined for German factories is significant: it suggests that the domination of the Ukraine was nowhere near as complete as the docile surface may have suggested. The local population was not so wholeheartedly in tune with their masters that they were prepared to believe promises of a better life in their country. Instead, the Kievans were forced on to the trains at gun point.

On 31 May the Botanic Gardens reopened and on the first day, more than 2,000 people came to visit. The reason so many people were able to visit was that on the same day that the Botanic Gardens reopened tram services were restored to the city, with six routes now running again. The Kievan resistance stirred. It established an 'underground railway' to spirit people designated for slave labour out of the city. The restoration of the trams provided the underground with a perfect way to get people out of the city in plain sight. They would put one or two people on to a crowded tram which could take them to the city limits. From there they could, with luck, vanish into the woods to join the partisans or make their escape altogether. By the spring of 1942, among the nationalist sector of the population there was, at best, a deep distrust of the Germans which increased when the nationalists started to be executed alongside the communists, and among the residual communists there was an outright hatred of the occupying force. The conquest of Kiev may have been the worst military defeat in history, but to the communists in the city it remained a temporary reverse.

The appearance of tranquil ordinary life was sustained by officially sanctioned and enforced civic events. To celebrate Hitler's fifty-third birthday on Monday, 20 April 1942, all of the Orthodox churches in Kiev were ordered to hold thanksgiving services for 'the liberator of the Ukraine'. There was also a special parade on the square in front of the university to mark the occasion. The propaganda photographs would show enthusiastic residents celebrating this great occasion, but realistic pictures taken by the Ukrainian underground tell a different story. There is a large crowd, but those on the fringes furthest away from the Germans, show the real feelings of the people of Kiev. They show faces that look sullen and resentful. Their eyes downcast, their gaze fixed anywhere but at the platform party, these are people who are there because they are only too aware of the potential consequences of not being present. It is a completely manufactured occasion. Nonetheless *Nova Ukrainski Slovo* continued to pour out the good news about life under the Nazis.

Schools were reopening, according to the newspaper. The four junior classes for children under eleven – all that Koch would allow – began on 11 May. The bath houses were also open again and, somewhat bizarrely, the paper claimed that two flower shops and a kiosk in the Galitsky bazaar were now open and selling 500 roses a day in May. For anyone, apart from the Reichsdeutsche and Volksdeutsche, news of the busy flower stalls must have been like salt in a wound. The majority

121

of Ukrainians had scarcely any money for food. They had no need of roses. It is difficult to see this report as anything other than a propaganda lie.

The occupation of the Ukraine had posed a singular challenge to the German authorities. The Ukraine was, by quite some extent, the largest hostile territory they had had to occupy. Countries such as Austria and Hungary were not considered truly hostile – Hungary was occupied only in 1944 as a defensive strategy – and even in those which were hostile, such as France, the Germans had not had to subdue the whole country. During the spring of 1942, the Germans made a sustained attempt to convince the people of the Ukraine, and Kiev in particular, that life under Hitler was indeed a far more pleasing prospect than life under Stalin. This was a calculated deceit: the hope was that in winning the hearts and minds of the locals they could buy themselves time to carry out their policies of extermination and deportation. They had used similar tactics in Occupied France where they had allowed the reintroduction of a form of café society with the reopening of night-clubs and cabarets. The occupying Germans probably enjoyed the music but its principal objective was to make the Parisians more tolerant of occupation. In Kiev, food supplies gradually became a little more plentiful. Although food was still difficult to come by for many people, a fashionable café called the Banks of the Dnieper was opened and boasted a jazz orchestra. You could even get a fashionable haircut now. *Nova Ukrainski Slovo* claimed that there were fifty hairdressing salons working in Kiev by the end of May – a haircut cost three roubles, a perm thirty roubles, and a shave cost two and a half roubles. The curfew was also eased and the new military authorities, aware of the fact that many people were keen to travel in and out of the city, relaxed the rules on movement, allowing people to go to nearby towns and villages providing they had the proper papers.

There was one area more than any other where there was a better chance of winning over the hearts and minds of the local population. Sport and a love of physical culture were inextricably interwoven into the fabric of Soviet society. If regular sporting events could be provided, then perhaps the local population might be a little more biddable. They began their sporting propaganda war by announcing that they would be allocating 50,000 roubles – an astonishing amount of money at that time – to complete the sports stadium which had been under construction when Kiev had been taken. The stadium which was to have been named after Nikita Khrushchev would now be renamed the All-Ukrainian Stadium. It was due to open on 8 July with a programme of boxing, gymnastics and football. A nationalist football team called Rukh had been established and they would play against a team from a local German unit to help inaugurate the new stadium.

The man responsible for reintroducing football into occupied Kiev was Georgi Shvetsov, a former footballer who, above anything else, never missed an opportunity for personal advancement. Shvetsov was the younger of two brothers who were born in Kiev just before the turn of the century. Pyotr, the elder brother, was more academically inclined. He was fond of science and ultimately became head engineer at a power plant, where he worked for the Bolsheviks. Georgi's talents were more physical. He was greatly taken by stories of their grandfather who had died heroically in Bulgaria when the Russians had freed it from the Turks. Georgi was determined to match his grandfather. Physically he was a tall, broad-shouldered, immensely powerful man and soon made a huge success of his chosen career as a soldier. He fought with distinction and gallantry in the First World War and was awarded the George Cross, which was the highest order Imperial Russia could confer on a soldier. It was during his time in the army that Shvetsov discovered football during kick-abouts with his comrades-in-arms. Although he was big and burly, Shvetsov was also extremely well coordinated and turned out to be something of a natural. He came to the game late, in his twenties, but quickly took to it. He joined Kiev City, which was effectively his home town team, and played with some success. Very quickly his goal scoring prowess as an inside forward brought him to the attention of Lokomotiv and he became one of their star players. Fans loved the sight of Shvetsov powering his way through opposing defences as he headed for yet another goal. His enormous physical strength made it very hard to get him off the ball and the delighted fans nicknamed him 'Paravoz', which means 'steam engine'. The peak of his career came in 1923 when Lokomotiv won the championship of Kiev. A number of that team went on to play for Dynamo, but the club did not offer terms to Shvetsov. They felt that by this stage he was too old. Shvetsov took the snub badly. He was bitterly disappointed. He was already a war hero but football gave him the chance of real fame and popularity. The sting of being turned down by Dynamo remained with him and made him more determined to become a sporting success by other methods. At first he turned to refereeing, but he found very little success there. Shvetsov's nickname came from his unstoppable nature on the football field, but off the pitch he was every bit as forceful. He was an intolerant bully who was not noted for his skills in dealing with people. Shvetsov complained loud and long to anyone who would listen that his career was being held back by a Jewish conspiracy. It is a fact that there were four prominent Jewish referees on the books of the local football association, but the notion that they conspired to hinder Shvetsov or anyone else for that matter is surely only a reflection of rabid anti-Semitism. The sad truth as far as he was concerned was that such an abrasive character was ill-suited to refereeing, as must have been obvious to everyone except Shvetsov. Refereeing for Shvetsov was supposed to have been a stepping stone in pursuit of his real dream of being an influential sporting bureaucrat. He had many ideas and a boundless enthusiasm but his inability to work with others led to his failure to achieve the heights to which he felt entitled.

When the war had begun in June Shvetsov was a sports instructor with the 6th Railway Regiment which was stationed near the village of Grushki, not far from Kiev. Unlike many of his fellow instructors and the other soldiers he did not seem to be too concerned about the prospect of a German invasion. Very soon after the beginning of Operation Barbarossa he simply disappeared and returned to Kiev to wait for the Germans to arrive. Once the Germans had taken over the city, Shvetsov suddenly had a Pauline conversion and became a fervent Ukrainian nationalist. He was, as far as the Germans were concerned, a model citizen. But all the time he was paying close attention to what was going on in the city and merely waiting for the opportunity to realise his thwarted dreams. The most obvious sign of Shvetsov's change of political affiliation was that he stopped speaking Russian in favour of Ukrainian. It had always been a bone of contention among Ukrainians that they effectively had to be bilingual if they were to succeed. They could only prosper under the Bolsheviks by speaking Russian, which meant they had to abandon their own language. Under the Germans, however, people at least felt free to express their devolutionary sentiments through their own language.

Shvetsov was a regular and sympathetic reader of *Ukrainski Slovo*. Even when it was purged and replaced with *Nova Ukrainski Slovo* Shvetsov did not waver since the new paper was broadly in line with his own feelings inasmuch as it remained anti-Russian, anti-Jewish and anti-Polish. Although it was in effect little more than a propaganda rag, Shvetsov could see the advantages in working for it. Before the war Shvetsov had done a little writing and now fancied himself as an influential sports journalist, a position of some status in society. He was an acquaintance of K. F. Shtepa, a professor of history and the rector of the University of Kiev, who edited the newspaper. Shvetsov traded on that acquaintance and was able to get a job as a journalist. It was not uncommon for Soviet sporting heroes to go on to become influential journalists and administrators. This is the path which Shvetsov had mapped out for himself, but his lack of sophistication was to be his undoing. Shvetsov was so determined to make a name for himself that many of his articles were little more than hysterical polemic. Unfortunately for him he did not have the wit to seek the protection of anonymity or a pen name. He published the articles under his own full name and, although he survived the war, his ego cost him many years in the Soviet labour camps afterwards.

The journalism was just one dimension of Shvetsov's two-pronged attack in his determination to reach a position of influence and power. As well as writing his newspaper articles he also organised a football team from other like-minded individuals who were in sympathy with the Fascists. He named the team Rukh which is a traditional Ukrainian nationalist term meaning 'movement'. However, he was frustrated that Rukh did not attract anything like the quality of players he had hoped for. Shvetsov was player-manager but, apart from himself, there were very few players of any real ability. Rukh was a team based on political affiliation rather than footballing talent and they were far from popular because of their overt affiliation with the occupying German power. They played their games in the old Dynamo Stadium which the Germans had renamed Deutsche Stadium and closed to the locals. Shvetsov, working through Professor Shtepa, convinced the city authorities that this was a mistake. A compromise was reached and the ground was eventually renamed Ukrainian Stadium. Even so when Rukh played there the crowd was mostly German with a smattering of local nationalists, because so-called untrustworthy elements were barred from entry. Naturally, these untrustworthy types included the former Dynamo players who, as prisoners of war, could not possibly be allowed to take part.

Famous in their own right, because there were so few young men left in Kiev, Trusevich, Kuzmenko and Nikolai Korotkykh were doubly conspicuous. Shvetsov realised the propaganda potential of having these communist sporting heroes in his Quisling side. However, no matter what kind of inducements were offered, none of the Dynamo or Lokomotiv players who eventually found their way to Iosif Kordik was willing to betray their principles or their team-mates by signing for Rukh, even though it would have guaranteed a significant improvement in their lifestyle and immediate prospects for survival. Only two players – Nikolai Golembiovsky and Lev Gundarev – played for both teams. Neither of them was particularly well known or influential and neither had any great sympathy with the communists. Whether or not they were OUN members is not known. Their politics were much closer to Shvetsov's. Gundarev, for example, was particularly harsh in his treatment of the wives of those Dynamo players who had escaped the encirclement and were still fighting. He destroyed their flats on official raids and helped root out those whom he deemed to oppose the new regime. Golembiovsky was little better. He became an interrogator and also helped the Germans in their persecution of the local people.

By the time Rukh was established, Kuzmenko and Korotkykh had joined Trusevich and the others at the bakery. Originally they had been living – most of them illegally – in various parts of the city but as more and more of them joined the workforce they found places in the dormitories in the relative safety of the factory buildings. They would work long hours in the maintenance crews but as soon as they had finished work they would go and get a ball and start an informal kick-about to entertain the other bakery staff with their skills. Iosif Kordik was delighted with all of his sportsmen and women for the measure of reflected glory and spurious respectability they bestowed on him, but he was especially proud of what he came to consider his 'team'. Eventually he persuaded the German authorities that it would be good for morale if they were allowed formal training sessions. The Germans, eager to press on with their pacification by normalisation programme, saw the wisdom in this and agreed. By this stage, Kordik had assembled an impressive array of players at 19 Degtyarevskaya Street. Thanks to that chance meeting with Trusevich he had managed to bring together some of the finest players in the Ukraine – the whole Soviet Union for that matter – as his yard crew at Bakery no. 3.

Trusevich was the key to the team. Not only a superb goalkeeper, the best in the USSR, he was the talisman for this group of players. He was the one who had brought them together, he was the one who buoyed them with his jokes and good humour, and, despite his easy-going manner, he was fiercely committed to their cause. Trusevich was the one that Shvetsov would have wanted more than any other for his Rukh side, because he knew that if he had him the others would come along too. But the goal-keeper, who never let a day go past without thanking his good fortune in having moved his wife and daughter to safety, was implacably opposed to the Germans and resisted every one of Shvetsov's blandishments.

Forming up in front of Trusevich was an impressive array of gifted sportsmen. Alexei Klimenko was the youngest and despite his boyish good looks he was a venomous defender. He was fast, he was athletic, and the ferocity of his tackles belied his slight build. His fellow defenders were Mikhail Sviridovsky and Fyodor Tyutchev. Although they had technically retired from the game – Sviridovsky, who was also the *de facto* coach of the team, had played in the 1932 Kiev side – they had correctly seen Trusevich's offer as a lifeline and grabbed it eagerly. With fellow veteran Mikhail Putistin from the 1936 silver medal side they were the oldest members of the team. They were still fit however and had lost none of their basic skills. They would not have considered themselves older, simply more experienced.

Men such as Nikolai Korotkykh, previously a shadowy figure on the fringes of the squad, now were finally given the chance to show their mettle. Korotkykh had been in and out of the Dynamo side for the past ten seasons, partly because he was often away from the city on official business. He was an attacking midfielder who was not selected very often for the first team. This was a constant source of irritation to him since hardly anyone paid any attention to the reserve team fixtures. He was a very good player, but he was in a squad of exceptional players in that pre-war Kiev side and so he found he did not play as often as his talent deserved. Eventually he was farmed out to Rut Front, a team from the local Polytechnical Institute, for the 1939 season. Rut Front was managed by Stephan Sinitza, one of Kiev's earliest players, and in that season, with Korotkykh in the team, they won the Kiev Cup. Now, once again, Korotkykh found himself among a squad of exceptional players, but this time he would have a chance to shine.

It was among the forwards that Trusevich had found strength in depth. As well as Nikolai Makhinya, who had scored Kiev's only goal in the first game of the 1936 championship, he had also located Pavel Komarov who had been Dynamo's top scorer before the war. His critics felt that Komarov lacked courage and would hold back from the 50–50 ball, but he had a striker's instincts and was a natural goal scorer. Komarov's lack of physical presence was more than compensated for by his striking partner Ivan Kuzmenko. He was frequently listed among the best players in the Soviet Union and in the championship immediately before the war 'Vanya' Kuzmenko had scored fifteen goals. He was a huge man, friends described him as being like a Tartar warrior with hair that flopped in front of his face in a curtain-like forelock. Vanya had a shot like a cannon and could strike a ball almost from the halfway line. Not content to rely merely on his natural strength and power, he was also extremely conscientious and would work hard at developing his game. Konstantin Shchegotsky recalled how on one occasion some of the other Dynamo players hung back after training to watch Vanya. They watched as he painstakingly sewed three deflated footballs inside each other before blowing them up and practising with a ball which was now three times heavier than regulation weight. Vanya reckoned that after training with this heavy ball, he could strike the match ball that much harder. Kuzmenko was also a man of tremendous courage to match his physical strength. There was nothing he would not do for the team. In one vital match against Dynamo Tbilisi, Kuzmenko had injured his foot but there was no one else to take his place. The manager asked him if he would play on and he agreed. Kuzmenko rooted around in the changing room until he found a boot which was two sizes larger than his own. He put this over his injured foot, tied it as tightly as he could and went back on for the second half.

Kuzmenko provided the strength in the squad, but it was Makar Goncharenko – the winger who had so carefully saved his boots in the certainty that he would play again – who provided the flair and the cutting edge. Goncharenko was compact and hard to knock off the ball because of his low centre of gravity. He was incredibly quick and fans had become used to the sight of him weaving his way through floundering defences as he searched for a pass to a team-mate or the opening for a shot for himself. Like all truly gifted players Goncharenko was blessed with extraordinary vision and anticipation. When he had the ball at his feet he seemed able to see his team-mates, not as they stood, but where they would be in about half a second. He could be relied on to deliver the ball to Kuzmenko or Komarov exactly where they needed it. Where Kuzmenko was something of a blunt instrument, Goncharenko was an artist. His shot was not hard, but it was precise and seldom inaccurate. His team-mates had become so used to Goncharenko's free-scoring habits that whenever he got through one on one with the goalkeeper they would simply turn and head back to the centre circle and wait to hear the referee's whistle announcing the goal. They were seldom proved wrong.

On top of all of this talent from Dynamo there were

also the players from Lokomotiv to strengthen the squad. Men such as Mikhail Melnik, Vladimir Balakin and Vasily Sukharev were equally well known with footballing reputations to match those of the pre-war Dynamo players. There is no doubt that Iosif Kordik knew that he possessed a formidable squad of players and when Georgi Shvetsov managed to persuade the Germans that they should reintroduce an official football season it was inevitable that Kordik would enter a team. The side needed a name and they decided to call themselves FC Start. The name in Ukrainian Russian is as prosaic as it is in English, the word means exactly the same in both languages. It is a very common name for sports clubs of all disciplines and may symbolise a new venture, something getting off the ground for the first time. It is also, given the tradition of naming sports clubs after organisations or societies, apolitical which may have had an underlying significance here.

The Germans finally announced that football would be resumed and the new season would begin on 7 June 1942. The first official fixture would be a match between FC Start and Rukh.

# CHAPTER EIGHT

The beginning of the first organised football championship in the Ukraine for almost three seasons was a significant development as far as the Germans were concerned. There was no league as such, the teams from Start and Rukh as well as sides from the various German garrisons – six teams in all – would take each other on in what was effectively a series of exhibition matches. The season was due to start on Sunday, 7 June 1942, and the occupiers were determined to make as much capital out of the summer sports season as possible. They had a policy of non-interference where sport was concerned, but that did not stop them from taking the credit for, as they saw it, yet another improvement in the quality of life under Hitler. The Germans decided to make the day into a carnival at the Ukrainian Stadium. The weather was glorious and the curfew had been relaxed so that the game between Start and Rukh could kick off as late as five-thirty in the afternoon. Naturally Georgi Shvetsov, writing in *Nova Ukrainski Slovo*, was all in favour of the event.

With the permission of the Stadtkommissariat and the help of the municipal authorities, our sporting life is coming back to normal. The first football team, which is called Rukh, has already been set up and various clubs are being set up at different factories and military units. For example, the bakery has already established a football club which contains some of the best football players in the city. On Sunday, 7 June at 1730 in the Palace of Sport a game will take place between Rukh and the bakery, and at 1400 a game will take place between the headquarters regiment of Luftwaffe and a team from the supply services of one of the divisions. Admission is free.

Echoing Shvetsov's newspaper article, posters in both German and Ukrainian were pasted up all over the city to announce the game. It was bound to attract attention, since it was the biggest distraction from the war to be offered to the general population in months. Admission was also free, so those who were not working could take some refuge from the drudgery of their lives by going along to watch a football match.

The team from the bakery had, however, not taken lightly the decision to play. There were those among the players – Makhinya, in particular – who felt that what they were doing could be seen as a form of collaboration. With his strong Stalinist feelings, Makhinya argued that they should not play and they should be prepared to accept the consequences. Equally there were those who felt that by playing they could do something to lift the morale of the people of Kiev, especially if they played well. The debate was conducted between a group of men who had come to know each other well. They worked together, trained together, rested together. Although it had been only a matter of weeks since Trusevich had begun to recruit the players of FC Start, already, an intense camaraderie, born of their extraordinary circumstances, had developed. In any football team players tend to gravitate towards a natural leader, usually this is the captain. The Start players tended to pay most attention to two players – the veteran Putistin, who had been a member of the great 1936 team, and the mercurial Trusevich. Putistin could be relied upon to bring a cool head to a situation, while everyone was aware of Trusevich's domestic situation and his hatred for the Germans. Together they could be relied on to provide a balanced view. But for this crucial fixture it was Trusevich who settled the argument not with rhetoric but with something overlooked in the fall of Kiev that he and Putistin had discovered in the ruins of a warehouse.

The bulk of the players in front of him were from Dynamo Kiev; some were veterans like Putistin, some were relative newcomers like Kuzmenko, and some were former fringe players like Korotkykh. But there were also the three players from Lokomotiv – Melnik, Balakin and Sukharev – who were every bit as famous as most of the former Dynamo players. As they assembled in the garage at the bakery to decide what to do, it was Trusevich who revealed what he and Putistin had discovered in the warehouse: a set of red woollen football jerseys, incongruously abandoned in the rush to escape the German invaders. No one knew which team they had once belonged to, plainly they were not from Dynamo since their colours were blue and white, but the two senior players, Trusevich and Putistin, spread them on the floor in front of the squad.

'We do not have any weapons,' Trusevich told them, 'but we can fight with our victories on the football pitch. Mikhail and I will wear these shirts. For a while the members of Dynamo and Zheldor will be playing in one colour, the colour of our flag. The Fascists should know that this colour cannot be defeated.'

It was a simple speech of great emotional power. FC Start would take part in the championships and they would play in red. Trusevich himself had found a heavy black jersey edged in red which would serve as a goalkeeper's top.

For Georgi Shvetsov the game offered the chance to offload the resentment against Dynamo which stretched back almost twenty years to the day when they had refused to sign him because he was too old. He was too old but, as he had proved in his ranting over the 'Jewish referees conspiracy', Shvetsov was never one to allow the truth to get in the way of a prejudice. He now found himself in a position where he could settle old scores on the opening day of the season. Not only would he have his revenge on a team composed largely of his old rivals, he would have it in front of the city's new rulers with thousands of Kievans looking on. This great victory would doubtless increase his chances of prospering as an influential sports administrator under the new regime. Shvetsov must also have believed that Start would be no match for his own team. As nationalists living in the general population, Rukh had a great deal more freedom than the bread factory workers of Start who were prisoners of war. While Start would be labouring in the bakery on a twenty-four-hour shift cycle, the Rukh players would have regular jobs with plenty of time off. Start were poorly equipped. Apart from the jerseys the rest of their kit was a makeshift affair. In place of shorts they would have to improvise from trousers, cut-down or otherwise. Goncharenko had boots, but the others had not been so certain they would ever need them again. Work boots, everyday shoes, canvas shoes, anything they could find in whatever size they could find it, would have to be pressed into service. Rukh had full kit and they would also be better fed, better rested, and generally in better shape than the Start players. On balance the Rukh side was also younger and fitter than most of the Start players.

The situation changed dramatically when the Romanian referee blew his whistle to start the game at half past five. Regardless of their physical condition, there was no getting away from the fact that Start were a vastly technically superior side. The nationalists may have been faster and fitter, but Start were a team. They relied on their basic skills and the understanding which had grown up among them during their after-work kick-abouts. The much less experienced Rukh side spent most of the game chasing them around the pitch with little to show for their efforts. By the end of the game Start were coasting. Goncharenko was in his element dribbling his way through the Rukh defenders, again and again leaving them in disarray. Start won easily with a final score of 7–2. Shvetsov was furious and humiliated after the game. His grand plan had collapsed at almost the first hurdle. His reaction was typically petty. He went straight to the city commander, Major-General Eberhardt, and demanded that the stadium be closed to the Start players, arguing that true patriots could not be expected to mix with prisoners of war. Eberhardt, who really did not care as long as it was only two Ukrainian teams beating each other up, gave in and agreed. He also gave Shvetsov permission to recruit to Rukh those Start players who were not considered especially untrustworthy. Naturally, Shvetsov targeted the big name players with promises of places to live and better food but, as they had before, they turned him down.

Even though his team had been humbled by them on the football pitch Georgi Shvetsov had still managed to do some damage to Start. Without access to the Ukrainian Stadium they had no place to train or play apart from the bakery yard. This could mean that they might have to withdraw from all the other games and forfeit their matches. At this point Iosif Kordik came to their rescue. Although he had brought them together, Kordik took little part in the day-to-day running of the team. That was left to a man called Grigory Osinyuk, about whom little is known other than that he was the Director of Sport at the bakery. It was Osinyuk who ran the training sessions along with Sviridovsky and dealt with the players on a daily basis while Kordik got on with the job of running the bakery. But Kordik was plainly a skilled negotiator. He had after all been able to pass himself of as Volksdeutsche so that he ended up in charge of the bakery, and he was more than a match for Shvetsov. Just as Shvetsov had persuaded the authorities to bar Start from the Ukrainian Stadium, so Kordik persuaded the authorities to give them the use of another one. Kordik believed in the virtues of sport and exercise as an antidote against the will-sapping routine of working twenty-four hours in the factory. It seems that he hoped to persuade the new rulers of Kiev that their working conditions were too harsh and could be tempered by encouraging other pursuits. Again, the military regime could not presumably have cared less about this minor local dispute, but in the end Kordik was able to take his team to the tiny Zenit Stadium adjacent to a public park in the middle of Kiev. It was here that Start would train and, beginning with the second game of the season, this was where their matches would take place.

The second game of the season was against a team from the Hungarian garrison. Hungary was allied to Germany, having signed the Tripartite Pact – the one with which Hitler had seduced Stalin in 1940 – to establish the new world order. Hungary had signed at the same time as Romania and although there were Hungarian and Romanian troops fighting as part of Operation Barbarossa they were there out of expediency rather than political ideology. Their governments may have been allied with Hitler, but for the soldiers at the front this was merely a decision taken by politicians. There was no real philosophical or sociological kinship between the Hungarians or the Romanians and the Germans. They had much more in common with the Ukraine in terms of culture, philosophy, lifestyle and even shared borders. Even so, the Hungarian side had been ordered to play the game and the fixture would have to be fulfilled.

There was no sign in this match of the Hungarian magic that would bewitch the footballing world in the

1950s. The garrison team were a very poor side with, apparently, no one who had played the game at any significant level. Start christened their new home at Zenit with a 6–2 win against the Hungarians on 21 June. Again Start dominated the game from beginning to end and one observer suggested later that the two Hungarian goals had been offside but the referee had let them stand out of an attack of conscience. A few days later, also at Zenit, the Romanian garrison were the visitors and they, too, were comprehensively beaten, this time by a scoreline of 11–0. The Start players would later suggest that the Romanians seemed not to mind. Indeed, Start found willing converts among many of their players and fans, who turned up to support Start in their subsequent fixtures. Start were building up something of a reputation. *Nova Ukrainski Slovo* would announce the games in advance and give them a lot of publicity to make sure there was a crowd but, curiously enough, the results were usually buried at the bottom of a column. Match reports and details of these first few games are consequently difficult to come by. This apparent attempt by the nationalists to suppress their communist rivals did not, however, stop the city slowly waking up to the fact that Start were a skilful side who played very entertaining football and were showing signs of being very difficult to beat. The news of each victory spread through the city and when people gathered together and the conversation turned to football the success of FC Start was invariably mentioned. Every win brought another boost in morale for the people of Kiev. Even imposing a fairly hefty admission charge of five roubles was not enough to deter the crowds from turning out in ever increasing numbers.

For the ordinary men and women of Kiev, the team made a genuine difference to their lives. A lorry driver, a man with no political axe to grind, who had been a boy of twelve when he lived in Kiev during the occupation, recalled what it had been like.

I lived with my mother at 22 Degtyarevskaya Street and I often went to Kerosinnaya Street where the stadium was to see how our team played. Because it cost so much to get in we would usually climb over the fence. It was hot that summer and the games usually started towards evening when it was not so hot. The referees were usually Romanians who spoke Ukrainian, German and Hungarian quite well. There were only ever enough seats for the Germans, so our supporters would always have to stand around the touchline or sit on the ground.

Trusevich would normally be terrific in goal and Goncharenko was great as a forward. You could usually count on Goncharenko to score a lot of goals in a game. I was amongst the local lads who would usually race to bring the ball back, which could often fly as far as Kerosinnaya Street. Our team would always win and the team from Rukh would always be defeated very badly.

The Germans had been quite content to leave the football to be run by the civil authorities. So far Start had proved popular, but their three victories had been against teams from other vanquished territories so there was nothing to be too concerned about. That, however, would change in their next game on Friday, 17 July 1942, when Start played PGS, a team from a German military unit, and trounced them 6–0. The Start defence had settled down – conceding only four goals in four games – and the forwards were scoring for fun as Start took their tally to thirty goals in those same four matches. Start were becoming something of a phenomenon and *Nova Ukrainski Slovo* could no longer ignore them. Equally, they did not have to make too much of them. For the first time, the newspaper carried a match report, but even in doing so they did their best to put as positive an interpretation on the result as possible for the Germans. The match report is signed only 'R.D.' and it is little more than an apology for the occupiers as it damns Start with faint praise.

It is impossible to describe this game as any kind of achievement for Start. The German side is made up of separate, rather strong, players, but you can not call them a team in the full meaning of the word. The side is made up of players who happen to be in the same unit simply by chance. You could also see the lack of training in PGS and even the strongest team cannot succeed without training sessions. Start, as everyone knows very well, is made up of players from the former Dynamo football team and for this reason we should demand and expect much more from them than what they showed in this match. The Kiev players ran offside more than ten times, which could be justified by the fact that the field was very small, but for some reason the German team did not have any offside.

The unfortunate R.D.'s report manages to give a pretty good account of things even as he tries to cast PGS in as favourable a light as possible. Reading between the lines, his report conjures up an image of a Kiev team who appear to have spent most of the game attacking the Germans in their own half of the pitch. PGS had no offsides presumably because they never managed to mount many successful attacks and when they did the Start defence was more than capable of dealing with them. The reporter also seems to be suggesting that Start had failed somehow in not having beaten the Germans even more heavily than they did. And having already obliquely cast aspersions on the Romanian referee, he goes on to adopt a familiar *cri de cœur* and blames the pitch for good measure. 'Why should such strong teams have to play on a small badly-equipped field where the grass is so thick that sometimes the ball gets stuck instead of going out?'

One thing R.D. did not take into account was that no matter how thick the grass or ill-prepared the pitch, for the Start players this untidy field close to a public park was still the Motherland. It would be fought for and defended just as heroically as if it had been Stalingrad itself.

In the midst of his complaining, however, R.D. did go on to point out that Klimenko and Sviridovsky had been outstanding, which suggests that a well-marshalled defence was the basis of Start's team philosophy of defending with vigour and attacking with venom. Regardless of the state of the pitch and referees who may have been anxious not to offend the Germans, judging from the scant match report the game seems to have been played in as normal an atmosphere as possible as far as the players were concerned.

In a radio interview recorded and broadcast in 1992, Makar Goncharenko looked back on that summer and remembered two things. The first was that, with the exception of one game, the Germans and their allies had behaved generally in a very sporting manner. There had, he recalled, been no deliberate fouling or attempts to cheat. Goncharenko also admitted that Start had done their best not to unnecessarily provoke the Germans. They would compete as hard as they could to win the game, but there would be no obvious attempt to humiliate or belittle the Germans. It seems obvious that the players on both sides were doing their best to set aside the politics of the situation and simply concentrate on playing a game of football. They were footballers first and representatives of a political ideology second. The game against PGS was something of a turning point in terms of media recognition for Start. Not only did the newspaper publish a match report there is also a picture of both teams after the game. It is a black and white photograph, but it is easy to distinguish the Germans in their white shirts from the Start players in their darker red shirts. All of the players who had become famous with Start are there.

Goncharenko is there at the end of one row, smiling broadly. Trusevich, the acrobatic goalkeeper who had kept another clean sheet looks happy, as does the striker Kuzmenko, looking slightly less burly than in his prime but still a potent force. Tyutchev, Timofeyev and Korotkykh are also there basking in the satisfaction of a game well won. Klimenko the young defender looks elated as does Komarov behind him, finally given the chance to prove his worth as a footballer. And right in the middle of the front row, proving that age is no barrier to experience, are the veterans Mikhail Melnik and the bare-chested Mikhail Putistin.

The expression on his own face and those of the other players bear out what Goncharenko said in the interview about the spirit of these matches. These are not the seamed and gaunt faces of men who are living under a virtual death sentence. They are flushed with exhilaration and exertion but they are smiling and taking delight in their own physicality. Even the Germans are smiling although, as the losers, their smiles are perhaps a little more forced. But the overall impression is not one of hostility. There is an ease and a comfort between these men. There are no obvious signs of antagonism here. The picture could just as easily have been taken after a Sunday morning kick-about as in the middle of the greatest armed conflict of the twentieth century. Uniforms had been exchanged for football strips; the men in the photograph momentarily were not soldiers or prisoners of war, they were simply footballers. Just like the famous Christmas Day football matches in the trenches of World War One, for ninety minutes the war and its consequences had been set aside. At Zenit Stadium there was only football.

Regardless of the generally sporting manner in which the games were being played, it is plain from Goncharenko's 1992 interview that Start were becoming more and more problematic for the Germans. A population which, if not entirely cowed, had been on the point of being docile had now found a rallying point in FC Start. The skill and vivacity of Start's play were winning them friends. It was not only the people of Kiev who were beginning to adopt them as their team, even their opponents were warming to them. After beating them so heavily, they now had a great many supporters among the Romanian garrison in Kiev. Start players remembered that Romanian soldiers used to bluff their way into the Start dressing room before games and smuggle food to them. They would then sneak out again after fervently wishing the Ukrainians well and encouraging them to make life as hard as possible for the authorities.

Even as Start were building up a growing support among the local populace, the Germans were still notionally maintaining their policy of non-interference. Privately, however, they must have hoped that Start might show signs of weakness and finally lose a game. Start were due to play another Hungarian team, MSG Wal, on Sunday, 19 July. Less than a month previously they had defeated a Hungarian garrison side 6–2, but this was reckoned to be an entirely different prospect since MSG were a much more skilful and better organised team than the one which Start had beaten earlier. They apparently had a number of players who had some professional experience and they were more used to playing and training as a team. In the end, Start won the game comfortably by a 5–1 margin. Again there was a match report from R.D. the following day in *Nova Ukrainski Slovo*. For once, Start were not damned with faint praise; they received none at all as, significantly, it was suggested that the victory had not been as comprehensive as it appeared. Indeed, according to R.D., it was not a fair win.

Despite the final score, it is not possible to consider these as two teams of equal strength. The Hungarians played most of the game with ten men because one of their players was injured and had to be taken off very early in the game. Start was once again saved by Sviridovsky and Klimenko. But even when the Hungarians found themselves in front of Trusevich's goal, their attacks were fruitless because they were one man short.

Start had won, but they had won against a ten-man team. At that time an injury to a player was an irreparable blow to a team. The rules of the game did not allow substitutes. So, having lost a man early in the game, it is no surprise that MSG were so heavily beaten. The result plainly rankled for a team who felt they were better than a 5–1 beating. Almost immediately after the game the Hungarian team officials went to the authorities and demanded a rematch. The game against MSG should have been the last of Start's season. The Germans, however, obviously heartened by the level of skill the Hungarians had shown and hoping that Start might yet be beaten, readily agreed to extend the season by another week. The game was scheduled for the following Sunday, 26 July.

Word had spread through the city about the revenge match and the crowds flocked to Zenit Stadium. Despite the five rouble entrance fee, set to deter the impoverished Kievans, the crowd was the largest at any of the matches

Start had played so far. Apart from the natural curiosity to see the return fixture from those who had watched the first match, there was another reason for the popularity of this game. For the first time, *Nova Ukrainski Slovo* had acknowledged the unique circumstances which had led to the team's existence in an article headlined 'Sportsmen of the Same Factory'.

The story, which was bylined A. Gavrilyuk, described these young people who worked at the bakery where the director employed not only football players but great boxers, gymnasts and swimmers. The article went on to claim that they could all take part in training sessions and compete in local events. But, it pointed out, 'the main pride of the bakery was its undefeatable football team'.

There were undoubtedly a great many people who had come to Zenit that day simply to see this phenomenon for themselves. Almost from the kick-off, the Start players knew that it was going to be a difficult match and their 'undefeatable' reputation might be in danger. For one thing it was unseasonably hot and even though the game was played in the early evening, the heat sapped the strength of players who were also working twelve-hour shifts at the bakery. The other factor which had to be considered was that, having played them already, MSG would know better than anyone how to deal with Start. The game was fiercely competitive and with a full-strength team MSG proved to be an entirely different proposition. Start were forced to play with all of the skill and experience at their disposal as they faced a side which was far superior to any they had met so far that season. They managed to take a 3–0 lead through goals by Kuzmenko, Komarov and

Goncharenko, but MSG would not give up. In the second half they attacked constantly and the Start defence, organised by the veteran Sviridovsky and young Klimenko, was under almost constant pressure. Ultimately, the pressure paid off when Start conceded a penalty and the Hungarians scored. The penalty gave them fresh heart and they scored again soon after. By the final stages of the match, Start were beginning to flag and the Hungarians attacked with renewed strength. It was only the skill of Trusevich in goal and some determined defensive play from Klimenko which prevented the equaliser. When the referee blew the whistle for full time, Start had hung on to win 3–2. They came off the pitch in a state of near exhaustion, but both sets of players embraced at the final whistle and were cheered to the echo by the record crowd as they made their way to the dressing room.

The epic contest and the tremendous win for Start was the last thing the Germans wanted. Not only had Start beaten the strongest team they had faced to date, they had also enhanced their burgeoning reputation as folk heroes in the process. Increasing numbers of Kievans gathered together just to talk about 'our team' and to relive in ever more epic terms Start's successes. The mood in the city was beginning to change and Start's accomplishments on the football field were having an effect on the city as a whole. Start were rapidly reaching the point where they were becoming an embarrassment. The policy of non-interference would have to be abandoned and plans put into place to deal with them.

Another football match had taken place in Kiev on 26 July 1942. Although to the ordinary citizens of Kiev the game which stirred the greater interest was the rematch between Start and MSG Wal, the other match was perhaps much more significant. While the crowds flocked to Zenit Stadium in their raucous thousands there was a much more subdued atmosphere at the Ukrainian Stadium. Just as Start played all their games at Zenit so Rukh had played all of theirs at the newly-completed national stadium. The nationalists were much less fervent in their support for Rukh than the communists were for Start, which reflected the gulf in the teams themselves. Most of the crowds in the Ukrainian Stadium were troops on leave who simply wanted to see a bit of football to break the monotony. On 26 July there were more troops there than usual to see Georgi Shvetsov's Rukh side take on a team called Flakelf. Some sources credit Flakelf as being the official Luftwaffe side, but this seems to be an exaggeration. As Hitler's Praetorian Guard the SS may have been the elite of Hitler's forces, the purest of pure-bred Aryans, but the aristocratic Luftwaffe were his shining knights of the air. By describing Flakelf as a Luftwaffe side the military authorities were trying to give them an air of invincibility. There were a number of pilots in the Flakelf squad, but the bulk of the side appears to have been made up of crews from the anti-aircraft batteries in Kiev as the name Flakelf suggests: the Flak eleven. Regardless of their personnel, Flakelf were described in *Nova Ukrainski Slovo* as a team which never lost and there was no doubt they were far and away the strongest of the German sides at that time. Other than the fact that Flakelf are known to have won handsomely, the score in the match against Rukh was not recorded in *Nova Ukrainski Slovo* or anywhere else. Other sources suggest that Flakelf not only won to maintain their unbeaten record but also won so comfortably that it seemed like a training game. Which is exactly what it was intended to be: it had already been decided that Rukh would simply be a rehearsal to sharpen Flakelf for a game against FC Start.

The football season had not included a single success for a German team and the authorities were eager that it be brought to an end as quickly as possible. They had wanted to pacify the locals so their agendas could be pursued unhindered, instead they had succeeded only in creating a talisman for the Ukrainians. With the war in the Soviet Union having already lasted more than six months longer than anyone had predicted and no immediate end in sight, this was an unacceptable state of affairs. Start's burgeoning potential as a rallying point for the Kievans would have to be stifled immediately and comprehensively. The simplest solution – to throw the players into prison or shoot them – would merely have left the Ukrainians with equally totemic martyrs which was no more desirable. Start could not be left any shred of mythic greatness. When they were destroyed it would have to be on the football field in front of their own supporters, and their destroyers would have to be German. Bolshevism had been trampled underfoot on the battlefield and now it would have to be ground into the turf on the football field. The season would be extended again, for another week, and there would be one more fixture.

The match between Start and Flakelf was scheduled for Thursday, 6 August 1942. The crowd was not as big as usual because it was a weekday, but there were a large number of Germans in the crowd. They had come to see their team prove their moral and physical superiority over these upstarts from the bakery. *Nova Ukrainski Slovo* was also on hand and primed to do more than its usual cursory match report. This game would be front-page news and the Germans wanted the news to be spread as widely as possible.

Start had one of their easiest games of the season so far and won 5–1.

# CHAPTER NINE

There were no official reports of Start's comprehensive victory over Flakelf and details of the match itself are impossible to come by, even so, the news of the 5–1 win quickly spread through the city . It was more bad news for the Germans at a time when they did not need any. On 28 July 1942, coincidentally two days after Start had beaten MSG Wal in the second game, Joseph Stalin issued his infamous Order no. 227 which has become widely known as 'Not One Step Backwards'. The previous summer, he had issued a similar order, his *Stavka* order, which had blared out from loudspeakers as the Germans rolled over Stalin's dead and dying troops when they poured into the Soviet Union. This time the order was different because it would be enforced with the utmost rigour. According to Order no. 227 'Panicmongers and cowards must be destroyed on the spot. The retreat mentality must be decisively eliminated. Army commanders who have allowed the voluntary abandonment of positions must be removed and sent for immediate trial by military tribunal.'

The order was meant principally for the Red Army

which was still reeling after another crushing defeat had led to the fall of Rostov. The German 6th Army was now almost at the gates of Stalingrad. As a consequence Stalin provided for the setting up of enforcement brigades whose sole order was to shoot anyone who deserted in the face of the enemy. These enforcement brigades were commonly in the second rank of major offensives to discourage anyone in the first rank from turning and running. Although high-profile acts of sabotage were no longer the norm, the underground and the partisans were still active in an intelligence-gathering role in Kiev in 1942. Some reports suggest that partisan troops had deliberately allowed themselves to be trapped in the encirclement to form resistance units. The new directive from Stalin was quickly circulated throughout the city by word of mouth. This was a key function of the Ukrainian resistance during the German occupation. They were able to relay information clandestinely to and from the city. Through the resistance men such as Trusevich knew that their families were safe and knew also that, whatever they had felt when the football season started, their efforts on the football field were being felt in a wider sphere of influence. The people of Kiev were being told by Stalin that for the sake of the Motherland they must resist by any means necessary and now with the success of FC Start they had a symbolic focus for that resistance.

It was Hitler himself who decreed that the physical perfection of the Aryan nation would guarantee their superiority in the sporting arena. His philosophy had been eloquently and powerfully articulated by the documentary film-maker Leni Riefenstahl in her 1935 film *Triumph of the Will*, a hymn to Aryan superiority. Riefenstahl also made the official documentary about the 1936 Olympics in Berlin, another supposed triumph for the Führer. In Berlin, Hitler had been embarrassed by the black American athlete Jesse Owens who had dominated the Games, winning four gold medals. Now once again the *Untermenschen* were proving the folly of Hitler's racist eugenics. The Führer's doctrine was being exposed by a half-starved team of a supposedly vanquished people. It was inevitable that this would be considered unacceptable.

Start had beaten Flakelf on the Thursday but by the following day hundreds of posters announcing a rematch appeared on shop windows, buildings, fences and lampposts throughout the city. Producing the posters in the first place was a very public admission that things had not gone well for Flakelf in the first match and the tone of the announcement removed any doubt that might still have existed in anyone's mind about the prevailing mood of the military administration. The handbill-sized leaflets were printed on the same drab grey paper on which all official announcements appeared. As before, the details were given in both Ukrainian and German and the populace were informed that on the following Sunday, 9 August, there would be another match at the Zenit Stadium in Kerosinnaya Street. However, underneath the word 'football' and picked out in the same size type was the word 'revenge'. Start and Flakelf were to play again and no one could be in any doubt that the Germans intended to win this game, no matter what it cost.

Whether by accident or design the choice of Flakelf as

the team which was intended to crush the upstart Ukrainians is an interesting one. Air aces such as Adolf Galland were the toast of the Fatherland as he and his fellow pilots had taken Hitler's blitzkrieg tactics to the brink of victory in Europe. But the Luftwaffe had singularly failed on the Eastern Front. They were overextended and forced to fly in miserable conditions which did not suit their aircraft. During Operation Barbarossa crippling losses had been inflicted on the Soviet Air Force which, thanks to Stalin's misplaced obduracy over the likelihood of a German invasion, had left its planes on the ground to be bombed. The survivors had fought with tenacity and skill. Later they would be reinforced with new planes from the United States and Britain, but even in mid-1942 Soviet pilots resolutely refused to surrender control of the air. The lack of German air superiority was a serious blow to the progress of Operation Barbarossa and one of the reasons why the fighting continued long after Hitler had supposed the Soviet Union would have been conquered. It was against this background that a defeated Luftwaffe football team suddenly found themselves being given a second chance. The 1942 football season was to be extended for one final contest.

In the seventy-two hours between the two matches anxious Kievans scoured every possible source of information about the game. The match was announced, as the others had been, in *Nova Ukrainski Slovo*. The citizens of occupied Kiev had grown adept at reading between the lines, but there were no clues to be had. The match would take place on Sunday at five in the afternoon and, the days of free admission long behind them, entrance would once again cost five roubles. The only other piece of information volunteered in advance – unusually – was the composition of the FC Start side itself. According to the poster there were fourteen players listed for the game – Trusevich, Klimenko, Sviridovsky, Sukharev, Balakin, Gundarev, Goncharenko, Chernega, Komarov, Korotkykh, Putistin, Melnik, Timofeyev and Tyutchev. The list of players is a curiosity and says a lot about how seriously the authorities had taken these games so far because it bears little relation to the sides which Start had fielded previously. Gundarev, for example, was a Rukh player who had only appeared once for Start, in the first game when the bakery side had struggled to make up the numbers. There are glaring omissions, too, not least that of Vanya Kuzmenko who was, along with Goncharenko, one of the most charismatic and best-loved players in the Start side. As well as the omissions, Start are also credited with fourteen players in their squad, which would have been something of a miracle for a team who had occasionally had difficulty finding eleven fit men. The poster's erroneous list reflects the fact that until recently Start had been largely ignored by the authorities and the little published information which had appeared was confined to the score and the briefest of match reports. It seems likely that those who produced the leaflets as well as the announcement in *Nova Ukrainski Slovo* did not really know who played for Start and the list was little more than educated guesswork brought on by the haste with which the announcement was made.

It is reasonable to assume that no one beyond the immediate German hierarchy in Kiev had cared too much about the results of the earlier games in the season. None of those matches impinged on the philosophy of the master race. Having taken over the city, they had gone out of their way to indulge the Soviet passion for sport with events which were designed to encourage the Kievans to have fun. They were supposed to be family days out, deliberately held on Sundays to provide a respite from the drudgery of the working week. A Sunday fixture also encouraged people to come along and fill the stadium. When Flakelf was beaten, and beaten comprehensively, attitudes changed and the football season suddenly acquired an overt political dimension. The policy of non-interference had been abandoned.

The Germans had been so determined to win the first game that they had done their best to kick Start off the park. This fixture had not been played 'in an appropriate manner', which was Goncharenko's tactful euphemism for Luftwaffe brutality. But the emphasis on physique rather than skill had not protected Flakelf from superior footballing ability and teamwork. Defeat for the Germans in the rematch was simply unthinkable. The Start players were certain that the harsh physical treatment meted out by the Germans in the first game would be repeated with even more vigour in the rematch. The referee in the first game, according to Goncharenko, had been so determined to see a German victory that he had ignored most of the foul play and there was no reason to assume that the referee in the second game would be any different. But in that first match even a referee who so clearly favoured Flakelf had been unable to protect them from defeat. There was no doubt, even allowing for their poor general state of fitness and the short break between the games, that Start could beat Flakelf again. But would they be allowed to? According to Goncharenko, the Start players had heard speculation that Flakelf were bringing in fresh players from all over the European theatre, established internationals who would only appear for this match. There were also suggestions that the Germans would no longer entrust the refereeing duties to the allegedly neutral Romanians who had previously been handling those chores.

The entrance to Zenit Stadium, appropriately for the gladiatorial nature of the contest it was about to stage, is neo-classical in design. The crowds thronging along Kerosinnaya Street passed first through a row of columns, then through a gateway set into a series of arches. It was at this gateway that they paid their five roubles. The admission price incidentally meant that anyone who had followed Start in all of their games would have had to pay out roughly half of their monthly wage. Even so, the game still attracted the biggest crowd of the season, larger even than the closely contested second game against the Hungarian side MSG Wal, which Start narrowly won 3–2. For the second game against Flakelf, the ground was full to capacity.

Zenit Stadium is set in a small hollow in the middle of a sprawling housing estate. Once they passed through the gate, the crowds walked down a long, tree-lined boulevard to get to the pitch itself, which lies in a natural amphitheatre slightly to the right as you come through the main gate. It is not difficult to imagine Zenit as a sports facility that enhanced the local community, a place where families might come on a Sunday afternoon for a picnic in the leafy grounds and to enjoy some sporting event or other. Although Start had ended up playing their games at Zenit as a result of Shvetsov's petulance, it was undoubtedly the perfect setting for the German notion of restoring peace through sport. At the end of the path a small flight of half a dozen stone steps took the spectators up to a slightly raised terracing from where they could look down on the pitch. The playing surface, which was indeed coarse and unmown as the *Nova Ukrainski Slovo* journalist had complained, was surrounded by a running track which turned the stadium into an oval. The only seating in the stadium ran down the length of one touchline. The seating was rudimentary, consisting of no more than benches like railway sleepers running the length of a raised embankment. In the middle of this seated area was a small grandstand. Like the seating, this was also a basic affair amounting to little more than a metal roof supported by six pillars. The floor of the grandstand was level with the top tier of the terracing and it extended about two metres down above a small wall built into the first few rows of the terrace to give its occupants an uninterrupted view. A small waist-high metal fence separated those in the grandstand from the hoi-polloi in the rest of the ground.

The games that had started as sporting carnivals bore little resemblance to the events on 9 August. There was little sign of family fun or festivity. As the people of Kiev began to make their way to Zenit Stadium on that hot Sunday afternoon the significance of the game could not have been lost on them. It was another stiflingly hot day at the height of a hot mid-summer. As the crowds thronged down the long path to the ground they were met with the sight of anxious-looking Wehrmacht soldiers stationed along the route. Dog handlers with powerfully-built Alsatians were also standing by to maintain good order. This was a new development, a clear sign of how seriously the Germans were taking this fixture. Anyone who had lived under German occupation had seen what these dogs could do when they were let loose, so everyone stayed as far away from them as possible. As the stadium filled up there was a strange mood in the crowd. The atmosphere was of suppressed anticipation. Makar Goncharenko remembers the Start supporters in the crowd as being nervous. They obviously wanted to see their team win again, but they must also have realised that another win for Start could lead to repression, perhaps violence, and the loss of the few freedoms they were now enjoying after almost a year of occupation. The Kievans who had arrived early in anticipation of getting a seat were disappointed. The terraces on the far side of the ground were filled with German soldiers.

The Ukrainians made themselves comfortable as best they could in the rest of the ground. The early arrivals sat on the grassy verge surrounding the running track while others stood at the back. As kick-off time approached and the crowds continued to pour in, those at the front moved on to the track itself to create more room. Only a few well-placed kicks from the German guards circling the pitch kept them back from the playing surface itself. There were no banners or chants and it seemed the only splashes of colour in the crowd came from the traditional twists of lace which the Kievan women wore in their hair. Regardless of the apprehension of their parents, the children could not suppress their excitement, especially the small boys. They still jostled for positions close to the touchline which meant that, not only could they see their heroes and maybe exchange a word, they might be chosen as ballboys. With no nets or perimeter fencing and men like Kuzmenko on the Start side, there was every chance of the ball sailing out into Kerosinnaya Street with a child scampering after it to retrieve it so the game could continue.

There was one other noticeable knot of activity in the crowd. Wherever Vladimir Klimenko sat there was always a crowd around him. It was not just that as circus performers for several generations the Klimenkos were among the oldest, best-known and most-respected families in Kiev. Vladimir was the oldest of the three Klimenko brothers. Alexei, who had performed heroics in the Start defence all season, was the youngest of the three. Vladimir had the energy and the physique to play football but he had been lame since childhood which prevented him pursuing his chosen career. Instead he became a potter and sculptor whose work had been much in demand before the war. Vladimir Klimenko was used to being the centre of attention as friends, neighbours and complete strangers gathered around to quiz him on the exploits of his younger brother and the rest of the team. Vladimir loved Alexei like a son and perhaps saw his little brother living out the life he would have wished for himself. Whatever the reason, there was nothing Vladimir, whom the children referred to as 'Uncle Volodya' using the affectionate diminutive, liked better than to talk about Alexei.

As the start of the game drew nearer, the crowd

gathered some confidence from its size and there were a few choruses of traditional Ukrainian folk songs. Well before kick-off the stadium could hold no more and it was taking the combined efforts of rifle-wielding guards, Ukrainian policemen with pick-axe handles and the dog handlers to keep the crowd from encroaching on to the pitch. Occasionally there would be a surge forward as someone stumbled at the back, creating a domino effect on the bodies in front, which spilled out only to be driven back by the Germans. Children fainting from the heat and others simply too small to see would find themselves passed over the heads of the crowds and helped down hand to hand to a better vantage point or simply a breathing space at the front.

The tension was also felt in the FC Start dressing room. Like everyone else, the players knew exactly how important this game had become. Any doubts about the German intentions in the game were swiftly dispelled by a knock at the changing-room door. Years later, Makar Goncharenko could still remember the man who came in. He was, according to the Start forward, tall and bald and dressed in an SS uniform. Two things stuck in Goncharenko's memory: the first was this man's impeccable manners and the second was his flawless Russian.

'I am the referee of today's game,' the young man told them. He spoke slowly, without raising his voice and carefully enunciating every syllable. 'I know you are a very good team. Please follow all the rules, do not break any of the rules, and before the game greet your opponents in our fashion.'

Although the tone of his short speech had been polite,

almost courtly, there was something unmistakably sinister in the deliberate, neutral tone he had adopted. There could be no mistaking the implication of the message to Goncharenko and the others. Start were not only being asked to play a supremely-fit, expertly-trained and well-fed German team who were packed with fresh legs, they would have an SS man for a referee. Moreover, the request to 'greet your opponents in our fashion' could only mean one thing. They were expected to begin the game with a Nazi salute, and they would have to shout 'Heil Hitler'.

After the referee had withdrawn there was uproar in the Start dressing room as the enormity of what he had said sank in. There were those who wanted to simply give in at once and abandon the game. There were others who felt that they should ignore the German's instructions and simply go out and play their normal game. One opinion was that they should try even harder and make sure they humiliated the Germans by beating them even more comprehensively than they had in the first game. The players were not the only ones who took a hand in reaching their final decision. There was a constant stream of visitors to their dressing room. Romanian soldiers again brought gifts of food and good wishes. There were also those who were urging caution in the face of the prevailing mood of the Germans. Some players from Rukh, including Lev Gundarev, suggested that perhaps it would be best for all concerned if they did indeed lose this match. Some city officials offered similar advice. They had done their best, they argued, they had had a good run and now might be a good time to simply let the Germans have their way and forget about the whole thing.

The Start dressing room behaved as any other football dressing room would. As kick-off approached, the visitors were firmly ushered outside and the players were left to contemplate their fate. A football dressing room before a match is a curious entity which has a life and a dynamic all of its own. It is the footballers' retreat from the outside world. It is perhaps the only place where they can close the door and be completely on their own. There are no secrets in the dressing room, everyone depends on everyone else. If there is a malcontent on the team, the others can spot him in the dressing room. If there are two players who do not get on, it is immediately apparent. And no matter how strongly or forcefully positions are argued in the dressing room, once the decision is made everyone abides by it for the good of the team. Football teams are run on a basis of collective responsibility. Start had begun its existence as a group of footballers who were grateful for the refuge which Bakery no. 3 had provided for them. In the nine weeks since their first game on 7 June, they had become a team in any sense that you cared to consider. Now they had a decision to make as a team. Those Dynamo players who had known Konstantin Shchegotsky had shown considerable team spirit back in 1938 when they refused to betray him to the NKVD. Since then they had been joined by other Dynamo players who had not been involved in that incident as well as the players from Lokomotiv. But still they had acted as a team. They had twice turned down Georgi Shvetsov when he had tried to lure them away with promises of an easier life, preferring instead the harder life they were already

166

living with their team-mates. Whatever they decided now, they would all have to live with the consequences, no matter what they might be.

# CHAPTER TEN

Shortly before five o'clock the teams emerged from the dressing room squinting into the bright but low early evening sun. Start were first out. The cinder track crunched under their feet as they were escorted through the crowd by the Ukrainian police. The crowds surged forward partly out of sheer excitement and partly to get a closer glimpse of their heroes. Those who got close enough would have seen that the ragged strips of two months ago had been replaced by something which actually looked more like a football kit. The red shirts were now augmented with red socks and white shorts which had been scavenged or donated by local people delighted to give something back to their team. Trusevich wore his favoured black jersey with red trim. Those like Goncharenko who had their own boots walked slowly, the studs on the boots giving them a slightly bow-legged gait. Trusevich and the rest of the Start players were wearing a strip which, at a glance, seemed identical to the national colours of the USSR. This, as he had told them when he produced the strips back in the bakery garage, was a colour which would not be defeated. The significance could not have escaped the crowd who would have fervently hoped that Trusevich's conviction was not misplaced. This was Flakelf against Start, but in the eyes of both sets of spectators it was also Germany against the Soviet Union, and Fascism versus Bolshevism.

The Start players trooped out and lined up in front of the high-ranking German dignitaries who had the grandstand to themselves, protected behind a ring of armed SS troops. One by one the players looked round at the ground which was full to bursting and tried to come to terms with the sea of people who had come to support them. While they were no doubt heartened by the sight of thousands of Kievans, they could not have failed to appreciate the sinister significance of one whole side of the ground being taken up by German soldiers. As the Start players gathered their thoughts and tried to concentrate on what was to come, the German side arrived on the pitch. The Flakelf players wore their usual white. The Ukrainian squad could see that there were some new faces among the Flakelf side. The rumours they had heard had not been true, it would have been almost impossible to transport German internationals to Kiev in the time they had available, even if they had wanted to. Nonetheless, the German side had been freshened up with men who looked every bit as fit, well fed and physically strong as those they had replaced. The Flakelf players drew themselves erect, clicked their heels smartly to attention, and with their right arms extended shouted 'Heil Hitler' to roars from the German section of the ground. The crowd waited expectantly to see what the Start players would do. As the Germans waited expectantly for the Ukrainians to comply, the Kievan fans had no knowledge of the instructions given in the dressing room. The Start players stood silently for a moment with heads lowered. This was their moment. They had made their decision. The pause was uncomfortably elongated. Slowly, and as one, they extended their arms. The crowd was still. The Start fans were puzzled, confused. But as their arms reached the apex of their salute the Ukrainian players snapped them to their chests and roared to a man 'FizcultHura!'

The teams filed away to the centre circle to start the game; the Wehrmacht were aghast and the Ukrainian fans elated. It was not until almost fifty years later that the story of what happened once the SS officer had left their dressing room that afternoon was made public. Makar Goncharenko recalled:

We listened to what he had to say and politely accepted his terms before he left. But, of course, we were never going to stand there meekly and shout 'Heil Hitler'. It is a lie incidentally that we prepared our strip especially for that day, it was the same as the USSR strip but we simply did not have another one. It was the strip Trusevich found right at the beginning and we always played in it, there was nothing sinister about it.

The choice of their slogan was significant. It is difficult to translate the word 'FizcultHura'. The word 'FitzcultHura' in itself means 'physical culture' in the sense of improving oneself physically and mentally for its own sake as opposed to sport which has a competitive and triumphalist element. Before any Soviet sporting event the participants would traditionally offer the greeting 'FizcultHura' to each other. The chant – a combination of the words 'fitzcultura' and 'hurrah' – means 'long live sport'. Not only was it a gesture of goodwill, it was also an affirmation that what was about to take place had a higher significance than the mere result. Under the circumstances there was no more appropriate rallying call.

Goncharenko was also able to shed light on one other persistent myth which has dogged accounts of this game.

No one from the official administration asked us to play weakly before the game. There were some other individuals who tried to encourage us not to irritate the Germans and cause any problems. We silently listened to their advice and then we decided for ourselves what we should do. We decided not to compromise, we would win but perhaps we would not win by too high a score.

Goncharenko argued with some justification that there was really no other option left open to Start but to play to win. They suspected, especially with some other players drafted in from other German military units, that Flakelf would be too strong for Start to dictate terms in the manner of previous games. There were no seasoned internationals, but it was obvious that the Luftwaffe side had been strengthened with good players from other units. The Start players also suspected, correctly as it turned out, that the referee would simply disregard any foul play on the part of Flakelf. Any attempt to answer in kind from a Start player would almost certainly mean a sending-off and that would effectively concede the match to the Germans. All FC Start could do was to try to win and win within the rules. Given that their players were seldom far from the point of starvation and had played an energy-sapping match against this team only three days before, this would be difficult enough in itself. Goncharenko pointedly remembers looking over to the Flakelf substitutes' bench before the game started and seeing almost another complete team full of fit, well-fed, superbly trained men, ready in white football strips and bursting with athleticism. He then looked across at the Start bench and saw only their trainer, Grigory Osinyuk. Flakelf had an entire team in reserve, while Start had only the men who were on the pitch.

Start did have one advantage which, probably more than anything else, had served them well on the football field in that summer of 1942. They had been left a valuable legacy by their former coach Mikhail Butusov, who had given them a system and style of play which turned out to be almost perfect for the conditions they had faced. Almost since the club was founded, Dynamo Kiev has been a vibrant example of the practical application of the latest and most sophisticated scientific and psychological theories as they apply to the world of sport. The modern Kiev sides are glowing testaments to the application of sporting science which was championed by their legendary coach Valery Lobanovsky, but this was a trend which was pioneered in the thirties by men such as Mikhail Pavlovich Butusov. His players remember Butusov with considerable fondness. He was a large man who was also apparently extraordinarily kind and extremely shy, but his eyes burned with a passion and intensity which spoke of his total love for football. If Dynamo lost, he could fly into spectacular rages – the players claimed he was like Peter the Great with his famous temper – but if they won or if they had played particularly well, he would rush on to the field to present them with roses. Butusov had escaped with his family just before Kiev fell, but his influence remained with his players every time they took the field in this most bizarre of seasons.

Butusov's last official game in charge had been a 2–0 win over Spartak in Kharkov on 16 June 1941, the last match in that truncated championship. For this game and some earlier ones, the Dynamo team had been playing a radical new system which had been devised by their coach. Butusov had travelled overseas the year before on a fact-finding trip to watch other teams and pick up new ideas from foreign coaches. It was in Spain that he noticed that the tactics that had served Dynamo so well at home were now hopelessly outmoded in comparison to those of teams from other countries. Butusov published an article called 'The Five Forwards' which outlined the deficiencies in contemporary Soviet football thinking. At that time Dynamo and everyone else played with five forwards in a line, which meant they could attack in strength. But, equally, half the team were liable to be left stranded upfield when the attack broke down and the other side launched their own counter-attack. Butusov championed the Western European system of two wingers, two inside forwards and a centre forward playing in a 'W' formation. He was the man who effectively introduced the midfield into Soviet football.

The 'W' formation turned out to be a godsend to the hard-pressed Start team the following summer. It allowed for the forwards to be supported from the half-back line when they were attacking, and equally it allowed for the defence to be reinforced by inside forwards tracking back and flooding what we now know as the midfield. Start would generally line up with Trusevich in goal and Sviridovsky and Klimenko as the full-backs. The half-backs would come from Tyutchev, Putistin, Melnik and Sukharev. On the wing Goncharenko and Korotkykh would link with inside forwards Makhinya and Balakin, to service the centre forward who would be Kuzmenko or Komarov. Kuzmenko was generally preferred because of his greater physical presence. It was the perfect formation for a team of limited resources, especially when those resources were themselves frequently on the point of exhaustion. The formation was both sophisticated and flexible and it was this combination which had allowed Start to achieve such comprehensive victories in their early games.

In this second game against Flakelf, the burden of expectation from both sets of fans at first appeared to be too much for Start to accommodate. The fullest account of the game comes in an interview recorded much later with Makar Goncharenko. He said the match started badly for Start and Trusevich seemed particularly distracted. The Start players had expected harsh physical treatment this time round and it was the goalkeeper who bore the brunt of it in the early stages. Every time he came for a cross ball or tried to come out of his area, he was knocked to the ground while the referee ignored the infringement. About ten minutes into

174

the game as Flakelf broke forward, Trusevich rushed out to dive at the feet of a German attacker. The Flakelf forward made no attempt to hold back or avoid the oncoming goalkeeper and instead simply left the momentum of his run unchecked and kicked Trusevich in the head, leaving him unconscious for several minutes. There were no substitutes available to Start and after he had come round the still groggy Trusevich insisted on carrying on. However, he was barely able to focus on the game for the rest of the half and it is hardly surprising that minutes after his courageous save, he was helpless to prevent the Germans taking the lead on their next attack. The Start players were outraged at the treatment being handed out to Trusevich in particular, but the SS referee, who, they noticed, had been visibly shocked when they had refused to give the Nazi salute, simply would not listen.

As they had done in the first game the Germans tackled hard, but this time they fouled even more directly. They tackled players after the ball had gone, they went into tackles with the soles of their boots raised so that their studs would damage an opponent's leg, they raked their studs down the back of the Start players' legs. They also simply avoided the ball altogether, going over the top of it and kicking the Start players in the shins. This left the Ukrainians, who did not have the luxury of shin-guards, lying injured all over the field. At set-pieces the Ukrainian players were bumped and barged out of the way and at corners they were blatantly held or had their jerseys tugged to stop them jumping for the ball. There was only so much of this that the Start players could take. They lacked the physical stamina to match the German tactics, their woollen shirts were heavy and sweat-soaked, and, weary from their exertions of the summer, they were nearing the point of collapse.

It was Kuzmenko who came to their rescue midway through the first half. Any time a Start player got near the Flakelf defence, he was hauled down mercilessly. Kuzmenko had the perfect remedy. The man who used to train with a ball which was three times the regulation weight picked up a pass from Goncharenko just inside the centre circle, he advanced a few strides, and then simply let fly from about thirty yards before any defender could hack him to the ground. The ball flew past the Flakelf keeper and Start were level. The Luftwaffe side were reeling at this departure from the game plan, at least as it had been explained to them. Start took advantage of the momentary confusion and began to move the ball around more fluidly. They were suddenly able to escape the worst of the challenges and despite the youth and vigour of the Germans it was apparent that Start were still technically superior. The Ukrainian ability paid off some moments later when the ball was slipped out to Goncharenko on the wing. The stocky winger, with his ability to anticipate opponents as well as team-mates, ghosted inside and evaded tackle after tackle. The defenders simply never got near him as he all but walked the ball into the goal. He had never been noted for the power of his shots, but on this occasion it was not an issue: he had scored a second goal. Start were inspired to greater heights, greater impudence. Just before half-time Kuzmenko sent a long ball through to Goncharenko who was playing on the shoulder of the last defender. The winger later remembered how he feared that if he even looked like going forward the referee would give him offside. Instead, he simply stepped back a pace or two and waited for the ball to drop and once it did he hit it on the volley with a shot which would have done Kuzmenko justice. A few minutes later the referee blew for half-time with Start 3–1 ahead.

The Ukrainian crowd could not believe what they had seen and they were understandably ecstatic. The celebratory roar had grown with every goal. The groans which greeted the Flakelf lead had long been forgotten. They sang and they cheered and they danced. Braver souls headed for the grandstand where, emboldened by their team's performance, they jeered and taunted the German officers and dignitaries. The response was to bring in the dog handlers. In other parts of the ground, sporadic fighting was breaking out between rival fans. A lot of the fans were soldiers who were on leave from the front, and they were spoiling for a fight after having spent most of the hot day drinking. The Ukrainian police and the German guards eventually separated them, but not before a number of Start supporters had been severely beaten.

In the Start dressing room the scene was equally chaotic. The jubilant players had achieved far more than they could possibly have hoped for. They had taken on the Germans and humiliated them in front of their own officers, but more importantly they had also done it in front of Start's own people. It was the crowning moment of the season, the vindication of the decision to begin to play under the occupying powers. There were half-time visitors, too. Following the example of the Rukh players who had come to see them before the match kicked off,

Shvetsov himself now appeared in the Start dressing room. For a man who hated Dynamo with a passion, Shvetsov was unusually conciliatory. It was not a question of lying down to the Germans in the second half, he told them, it was a question of protecting themselves and everyone else. Shvetsov seemed sincere in his appeals and left feeling that he had done his best. Some of the players felt he was only protecting his own interests, a defeat for Flakelf would be just as damaging for Shvetsov as it would for anyone else. A few moments later they received another visitor and the import of Shvetsov's argument became instantly clear. It was a second SS officer. Again he was polite and again his Russian was flawless. He told the Start players very pleasantly that they had played very well in the first half and that the Germans had been very impressed with their skill and their athleticism. However, he pointed out, they should understand that they could not possibly expect to win. They should take a moment to think about the consequences before they went back on to the field.

When the players came out for the second half they could barely hear themselves shout instructions to each other above the noise. The perimeter fence had now been replaced with a ring of armed guards who stood shoulder to shoulder facing into the crowd. The guards were so close to the touchline that the wingers were in severe danger of bumping into them as they played. Trusevich was particularly vulnerable after the treatment he had received from the German forwards in the first half. In the second half he was subjected to a torrent of abuse from the German fans, especially since he provided a static target between the goalposts. On the field the second half was something of an anticlimax. Both sets of players were shaken by the circumstances in which they were being asked to play. The tackles were no longer as physical because the Germans were as fearful of the Kiev fans as the Start players were of the German soldiers. Start remained the superior side and although both teams scored twice in the second half, there was no chance that Flakelf would threaten to win the contest.

Vladimir Mayevsky would go on to play with distinction for Dynamo Kiev in later years, but in August 1942 he was a ten-year-old boy who was taken to the game by his father.

I remember that the whole of the central part of the stadium was taken up by Germans. There were Hungarian troops standing on the hill on one side and the rest of the audience were standing along the perimeter of the stadium. I remember our team scored a lot. Our best players were Goncharenko and Klimenko.

Mayevsky remembered that the Hungarian troops were among those cheering loudest of all in the second half. He also recalled the final humiliation inflicted on the Germans by young Klimenko.

I remember he side-stepped all of the German defenders, including the goalkeeper. Then he ran to the goal line, but instead of putting it into the goal he stopped it on the line. Then he ran into the goal, turned, and kicked the ball back up the field and into play.

Enough was enough for the SS man in the referee's uniform. He blew for full-time, even though the ninety minutes were not up, to spare the Germans any further embarrassment. Start had won 5–3.

Start had beaten the pride of Germany in the Ukraine not once but twice in three days. They had embarrassed the German military command. And the man who administered the final insult, the man who spurned the chance to add to their disgrace by scoring a goal and in doing so humiliate them even further, was the youngest member of their team. And a defender to boot.

# CHAPTER ELEVEN

As the Start players left the field that evening they were not celebrating. They were quiet and almost sombre. They knew their victory was likely to have repercussions. The players left the pitch with only cursory handshakes and pleasantries. The Start players were more exhausted than elated and simply wanted to get back to their dressing room. The crowds continued to surge forward and once the footballers had left the field, the police and the SS turned the dogs loose to clear them. At the grandstand where the German high command had been treated to an uninterrupted view of a propaganda debacle, the officers and other dignitaries were mobbed and jostled by jubilant Kievans as they tried to make their way into the cars. The German guards had to fire their pistols into the air to try to bring some sort of order to the situation.

Perhaps surprisingly, given the savagery of the reprisals for other offences, there was no immediate retaliatory action after Start had beaten Flakelf for a second time. The Ukrainian players spent a very anxious few days after the match expecting to be arrested at any moment and shot for their insolence. Instead, they were allowed to go about their business as normal. They went back to Bakery no. 3 and carried on working in the yard and the dispatch area. They even continued to train whenever they could at Zenit Stadium and were even more surprised when Iosif Kordik came to them and told them that another fixture had been arranged for the following Sunday.

With hindsight it is perhaps not too difficult to see why the Germans did not do anything too precipitate. Senior officers had watched with their own eyes as every shred of superiority they had asserted during the previous year disappeared in less than ninety minutes. It was bad enough that the local population jeered and booed, but that they had been joined by soldiers who were supposed to be Germany's allies was humiliating. German mastery of Kiev was a fragile thing for the few days immediately following this football match. The native population was exultant and their blood was up. Stalin had told them they must not surrender and they seemed prepared to take his message to heart. The example of the Start players who had taken on and defeated the best that Germany could throw at them – not once, but twice in grossly unfair circumstances – was a touchstone for the Kievans. The people were no longer cowed as they had been two months earlier, they held their heads a little higher as they went about their daily business, and they could look the occupiers in the eye with a hint of defiant pride. Had the Germans simply stormed into the Start dressing room at the end of the game and dragged the players away, they would almost certainly have had a full-scale riot on their hands. The situation was already tense but giving martyrs to the crowds would be inviting disaster. Instead, the military authorities seemed content to wait. And so they extended the season yet again.

It was announced that on 16 August, one week after the game against Flakelf, Start would be playing Rukh in a rerun of the opening fixture of the season. Ever since that 7–2 defeat Georgi Shvetsov had been lobbying for a rematch. He had offered all sorts of excuses for his team's failure that day. He also claimed that since then Rukh had amassed an impressive series of results, which had earned them another chance at the undefeated Start. It is true that Rukh had won a lot of games but, according to Goncharenko, the quality of the opposition was desperately poor, consisting of the sort of makeshift garrison teams which Start had beaten comfortably at the start of their season. Rukh also included in their victories a game against another local team, Sport. This side, however, was made up of young local players who were not terribly good and far too young to compete seriously against a senior team. Start had previously refused any requests for a rematch by claiming simply that they had too many other fixtures to fit in. Now there was no such excuse. The game was scheduled for the following Sunday. The result was never in any doubt and Start won comfortably 8–0.

The atmosphere at this second match was considerably more muted than at any of the other games of the season. Things had become so quiet in the week since the Flakelf debacle that Makar Goncharenko genuinely believed that the row had blown over. This was unlikely. Some sort of punishment was inevitable and what Goncharenko mistook for calm may simply have been a period in which the authorities were making up their minds about the difficult choice of what to do next. The most likely scenario would have been to allow the game against Rukh to quietly bring to a close what had been a disastrous season for the Germans. They could then deal with the members of the Start team at their leisure. Whatever they had in mind, matters were once again brought to a head by Georgi Shvetsov, who behaved as usual like the steam engine which had given him his footballing nickname. Shvetsov could not bear the humiliation of Rukh once again having been beaten so comprehensively and disdainfully by Start. As he had done after the first game he demanded that action be taken. The Start players, according to Shvetsov, were flouting the authority of military rule. They were living far too freely and their very liberty was a constant affront to the Reich. In addition, Shvetsov pointed out, every day that these men walked the streets was another propaganda victory for the communists. He, as an ardent nationalist, could see that, so they should also be able to see it. Shvetsov's argument found some supporters among the occupying authorities, but he did not offer a solution to the dilemma about what response was likely to prove emphatic and effective. It seems likely that the German authorities were planning to sanction the arrest of at least some of the Start players, probably on a pretext of theft or sabotage or some other infraction of the draconian rules. Now Shvetsov, who for all his bluster and bombast was still an influential member of the nationalist community, was accusing Start of effectively making fools of them. The Germans could not ignore this kind of protest at such a delicate period in the war. The order was duly given for the Start players to be arrested.

Their performances on the football pitch had given the men who played for Start, already heroes when the war began, an almost mythic status in the city. People would risk punishment themselves to slip food to them or even simply to talk to them. They had been allowed their freedom partly as living testament to how completely Kiev had been subjugated, now, as Shvetsov quite correctly pointed out, they were a walking advertisement for resistance. The Germans took a pragmatic approach. They simply went to the names of the players who had appeared on the handbill for that last game against Flakelf and used that as the basis for their arrests. The list was refined with some names, such as that of Kuzmenko, who was not on the team list, being added while others, such as Gundarev, who was really a Rukh player and could be vouched for, were taken off. It seems likely that the Germans would have had some assistance in compiling the names of the detainees. The elimination of the Rukh player Gundarev's name from the list points to some involvement by Shvetsov. One by one the Start players were arrested.

Plain clothes Gestapo officers turned up at the bakery in Degtyareskaya Street and took over Iosif Kordik's office, which was situated on the gantry above the factory floor. The players were called, one at a time, to go and see Kordik. When they reached the office, Kordik was nowhere to be seen, a Gestapo officer was in his place. The footballer's name was checked against their list and the unfortunate player was bundled outside into a waiting car and taken away. The mood in the factory

185

became increasingly sombre. The workers must have anticipated something was about to happen because of the presence of the Gestapo. Their suspicions would have been further aroused when the names were called, one by one, over the tannoy, summoning individuals to Kordik's office. Each of the names called out was a footballer. The workers watched them walk up to the office, but saw none return to his work station. The inference was obvious. The player-coach, Sviridovsky, was the last one to be arrested. He was not at the bakery when the others were taken. He was spotted later refereeing a match between a couple of local teams, one of which he had been training secretly in return for extra food. He had no right to be doing this and so he was arrested on the spot and joined the rest of the Start players. Kordik was undoubtedly furious at the treatment of the men he regarded as his players, but he was too much of a pragmatist to take any overt action to prevent their arrests. Kordik would have realised that one more arrest would not inconvenience the Gestapo in the slightest. They could always find someone else to run their bakery.

The players were taken to the Gestapo headquarters in Korolenko Street. They were all placed in separate cells, but since the cells faced each other they could still see their team-mates, although talking was forbidden. One at a time they were taken in to be interrogated. The Germans wanted them to admit that they were thieves or saboteurs. If they had admitted that they would have been discredited and shot but none of them would confess nor would they inform on anyone else. Even at that early stage, there was one Start player who was singled out for special treatment. Korolenko Street was a daily torment for the other players, but for Nikolai Korotkykh it was an automatic death sentence. In the spring of 1941, when Hitler was putting the finishing touches to what would become Operation Barbarossa, he had drafted the Commissar Order specifically providing for German soldiers to shoot Soviet political officers out of hand without any pretence at due process. As a consequence of the Commissar Order, which flew in the face of even the most liberal interpretation of the Geneva Convention providing for the fair treatment of prisoners of war, any Soviet commissar or senior party official was invariably handed over to the SS for special treatment. Nikolai Korotkykh came into this category because, as his team-mates had suspected but never mentioned, he had been an active officer in the NKVD. Ten years previously when he was living in Ivanovo, an industrial textile town in Russia, Korotkykh had become a professional NKVD officer and served with the secret police for two years rounding up undesirables and implementing Stalin's hard-line policies. Most of the Dynamo players were nominally NKVD men themselves and it would have made no difference to them. They, however, were NKVD only by affiliation, in the sense that it gave them the right to play for Dynamo Kiev. They were footballers, pure and simple, while Korotkykh was a serving officer. His team-mates insist that, despite his other life, they knew him as kind and friendly and – which was most important to them – a good footballer. When the Germans discovered his past they might as well have shot him on the spot.

The exposure of Nikolai Korotkykh as an NKVD

officer is a tragic example of the reality of the situation in Kiev. In a cruel echo of the paranoia which had gripped the Soviet Union during the thirties, enforced by NKVD officers such as Korotkykh, he was betrayed, according to his widow Anna, by his own sister. None of his team-mates revealed any suspicion they might have harboured, but Korotkykh's sister was convinced that his active membership of the NKVD would be discovered during his interrogation. If he was revealed to be a member of the NKVD then not only would he be killed but there would be reprisals against his family as well. In an attempt to protect herself and the rest of her family, she volunteered the information about her own brother. It seems likely that the Germans had known about Korotkykh's status, if not for some time then at least before the games which followed the second Flakelf match. As soon as the team had been taken to Gestapo headquarters, Korotkykh was immediately singled out, which suggests the authorities had some suspicions. Trusevich, Kuzmenko and the rest were interrogated every day for three weeks. They were subjected to the German version of Stalin's Conveyor with teams of interrogators wanting them to admit to being spies or partisans or anything which would allow them to be 'legitimately' executed. There were three sessions of interrogation every day, never at regular intervals so the prisoners were disoriented and could not prepare for when they would next be interrogated. The constant questioning was punctuated by physical brutality. They were beaten savagely and regularly. The harsh bright lights were left on in their cells constantly, again making it difficult to calculate the passage of time. When they were fortunate enough to find some solace in sleep, the guards would burst in and wake them in the hope that sheer exhaustion would encourage them to incriminate themselves or their team-mates. Food consisted of a near starvation diet, even by their recent standards, of coarse black bread and some water. Hunger, it was hoped, would sap their will and force them to talk.

Throughout their nightmare the Start players were careful not to admit to anything and their strength as a team gave them added resolve. They were no more inclined to yield to the pressure of intense questioning now than they had been four years earlier when the Soviet inquisitors had demanded that they incriminate Konstantin Shchegotsky. The players, facing each other in their cells running down opposite sides of a corridor, could signal to each other to bolster morale and strengthen flagging wills. Korotkykh enjoyed no such luxury. He was removed from the others, as he must have suspected he someday would be, and was tortured without respite. On the twentieth day he died, tortured to death by the Gestapo. Two days later the interrogation of the other team members stopped. Still under arrest, they were taken from Korolenko Street to the camp at Siretz, near Babi Yar.

# CHAPTER TWELVE

Siretz was situated on the outskirts of Kiev, to the north-west, just beyond the ravine at Babi Yar. It takes its name from the nearby river, which is a tributary of the Dnieper. There was a time when Siretz had happy connotations for the people of Kiev. The original village had belonged to a local prince who had donated it to monks at a nearby Dominican monastery in the eighteenth century. For a time, in the first half of the nineteenth century, it was officially included within the boundaries of the city and was used as a summer camp to provide rest and recreation for the Kiev garrison. Latterly it had been used as a military airfield and was once again placed outside the city limits.

Regardless of how it was described at the time by the Germans, as a labour camp or a concentration camp or any other semantic distinction one cares to apply, post-war Soviet historians were in no doubt about the function of Siretz. It is described simply and un-equivocally as a death camp. It made no difference to the men and women who ran this institution whether the Start players were bakers, footballers or anything else.

Once they arrived at Siretz, they became nothing more than livestock in a human abattoir. They had effectively been condemned. They could try to eke out their existence as long as possible, but Siretz was a living hell with only one expected outcome. A great many people had made the journey from the Gestapo prison in Korolenko Street to Siretz, but very few returned.

In construction, the camp at Siretz was not appreciably different from dozens of other similar institutions dotted throughout Eastern Europe. There were two parts to the camp. There was an area which had been designated as living quarters and a second, larger, space which was the working part of the camp. When the Start players arrived in September 1942 the conditions in the camp were already atrocious and they would worsen steadily over the next few months. There was no hygiene to speak of. For the prisoners, water had to be brought manually from the river and there was no sanitation system other than the most rudimentary latrine. The stench in high summer was appalling and in this unusually hot summer of 1942 a foul miasma of disease and filth had hung over the camp for months. The prisoners lived in large barracks and slept on bunk beds ranked along the walls. The bunks were so narrow and so close together that there was barely enough room for a full-grown man to lie on one comfortably. The only reason they had enough space to turn over was because most of the prisoners were so rake-thin that they occupied only a fraction of the space they should have taken up. The barracks were neither ventilated nor insulated, which meant the prisoners almost suffocated in the stifling heat of the summer, while in the winter it was so cold that freezing to death was not uncommon. The German version of temperature control was as inefficient as it was uncaring. They simply had the prisoners dig huge holes in the ground which, with the rudimentary covering of a corrugated metal roof, became underground homes into which they were rehoused. Each of these so-called homes had to house around 100 people packed together in conditions in which you would not have kept farm animals.

The normal ration of food at Siretz consisted of a daily lump of coarse bread of between 150 and 200 grams, although the measure was usually closer to 150 than 200. The bread was old and hard and the only means of softening it came with a soup of reconstituted barley or coffee which, if the inmates were lucky, was made from acorn grounds. It was a diet completely lacking in minerals, vitamins, protein or anything else which was necessary to sustain normal life, far less one of constant physical toil. The Start players had an advantage over the other residents of the camp; as athletes they were in better condition going into the camp than most of the other prisoners had been. Starvation was the principal cause of death at Siretz as it was at other German camps. Every day at Siretz started the same way with a morning roll-call. Once the dead had been identified and taken away to be disposed of, those who were infirm or too weak from hunger would also be weeded out for special treatment, leaving the others to endure another day of numbing inhumanity. The working day at Siretz started at four in the morning no matter what time of year it was. After the roll-call there was the grotesque spectacle of the unfortunate inmates being put through a rigorous regime of physical exercises. Again this was something the Start players were used to, but for the other pathetic souls who were not so well conditioned it was another hurdle to be overcome. Those who were too tired or sick to complete the exercises but had managed to survive the cull at roll call were weeded out here and once again their fate was sealed.

After roll-call and exercises the prisoners were marched off to a day of harsh physical labour. The prisoners dug ditches or built roads, cut down timber or dug out tree stumps. Roped to vast tree trunks, teams of emaciated prisoners were used as draught animals and were beaten and cajoled as such by pitiless supervising soldiers. This grinding routine would go on until the end of the working day at six o'clock when those who still had the strength would make their way back to the camp for the meagre meal of bread and soup.

'We were not really fed at all in the camp,' one prisoner recalled later. 'Every day we were sent to do some more digging. You could study anatomy on our bodies, we were so thin. Those who could stand up were alive, the rest were killed.'

Siretz was run by Obersturmbahnführer Paul Radomsky. There is some confusion about Radomsky's nationality. There are suggestions that he was a Ukrainian; on the other hand, there are also reports that he had come from Hamburg where he had owned a power plant. Since he was a senior officer in the SS, it does seem more likely, given his position of influence in Kiev, that he would have been a German national. His deputy, Richter, whose first name is not mentioned in the records also appears to have been German.

According to *The Final Duel* by P. Severov and N. Khalemsky, published in the Soviet Union in 1959, Radomsky was, by all accounts, a heavy, corpulent man with an incongruous thatch of sandy red hair – his nickname among the inmates at Siretz was 'Red-headed Paul'. One account describes him as looking like a very well-fed chef. His eyes were watery to the point of being colourless, he was extremely overweight, and his double chin merged with his chest to give the impression that he had no neck at all. Yet, despite his appearance, Radomsky was also extraordinarily vain. He loved having his photograph taken in his dress uniform – one description of such a photo recalls him lovingly fingering an Iron Cross – and these photographs were then given as tokens to those subordinates whom he favoured.

Radomsky was never seen without his whip and his Luger. The gun sat at his waist, nestled beneath a gut which spilled over his belt, his plump hand resting on the flap of his holster, and the whip was carried in his arms. At his feet was his dog, Rex. The dog was an Alsatian which Radomsky had arranged to be brought especially from Hamburg and provided with special training. The dog had an appetite for raw meat which was hard to come by during the war, however Radomsky's special training provided a substitute. At a whistle and command from his master, Rex would snarl and slaver at a chosen inmate, on a further whistle, and let off his leash, Rex would then lunge towards the luckless inmate and savage him.

Radomsky was personally responsible for a regime of the most capricious and savage cruelty. Even the most minor infraction of the rules was punishable by death and Radomsky was responsible for creating a climate in the camp so depraved that the guards were encouraged to find new and inventive ways to torment and exterminate the prisoners. One favourite method was to send the prisoners up into a tree, then once they had climbed to the highest branches with guards taking pot shots as an incentive, other prisoners would be made to fell the tree. If the poor wretches in the topmost branches were not killed by the fall, they were simply left buried alive under the foliage. The guards maintained their superiority over the inmates by constantly demeaning and humiliating them. For example, the prisoners were not supplied with uniforms, they simply wore what they had when they came to the camp. As the duration of their stay increased their clothes became more and more tattered and ragged until many of them were nearly naked, a crude but highly effective way of demeaning them as men and diminishing their fighting spirit and will to resist. This psychological taunting continued as part of the daily routine at Siretz. As they walked from place to place or from their barracks to their work the prisoners were subject to the perverse idiosyncrasies of the guards. They would be arbitrarily ordered to run in circles, or lie down, or walk by taking only tiny steps. The guards would also frequently order them to lie on their stomachs with their hands behind their backs and move themselves along on their shoulders and knees. As the prisoners struggled to comply with the whims of their guards, they were also subjected to dreadful physical cruelty. Prisoners were subject to a constant barrage of kicks and beatings from rifle butts and clubs made from pick-axe handles as they vainly attempted to crawl along in the dirt. It was an exhausting and demeaning ordeal, but there was worse. Anyone who had the strength and courage to be able to get to his feet again after covering a set distance of around 200 metres in this manner was then savagely beaten. The guards referred to this as 'physical exercise'.

At the centre of this microcosm of obscenity was Radomsky himself. He personally administered the special treatment to those prisoners who were not able to force themselves through another day. Every morning after the exhausted and the infirm were set apart from the rest of the prisoners, they would be thrown into an underground bunker. At six in the morning there would be another roll-call among these prisoners. Those who were sick were asked to step forward. Those who did so were shot on the spot by Radomsky. The others were thrown back into the bunker where they were left to die without food, water or medical treatment.

The whip was a particular favourite of Radomsky's. During the day he would single out those he felt were shirking and not working sufficiently hard; others were singled out because they had done something to upset him. These people were whipped as often as Radomsky saw fit. Many of them were whipped until they died, either from bleeding to death or simply because their hearts gave out. Those who were still alive were thrown into the bunker with the others to await Radomsky's morning executions. He would carry out the shootings every morning at six and then repair to his quarters for breakfast.

The Nazis had such institutionalised contempt for their prisoners that on some occasions they did not even consider them worth a bullet. Some sick prisoners who could not work were savagely beaten senseless and buried alive, in the knowledge that if they did regain consciousness they would not have the strength to free themselves from their shallow graves. In winter, the sick were beaten and left outside to freeze. On some occasions they were not even beaten, they were just left in the cold to die. One report tells of Radomsky going into the underground bunker one morning and finding eight men who were so grievously wounded and so cold that their limbs had frozen. They could not move. Nonetheless, Radomsky had them dragged out of the bunker and into the yard where he shot them.

The prisoners at Siretz lived in a constant state of suppressed terror. They lived a life where they knew that their next breath could be their last. Their lives were entirely at the disposal of Radomsky and his soldiers and they were absolutely subject to his whims. For example, a rule was introduced which made it compulsory for every prisoner to smile when talking to or greeting a member of the Gestapo or the local police. Anyone who did not smile would be shot. In the woods where they carried out their logging operations, any prisoner caught trying to eat anything, whether it be an apple or a handful of leaves, could be shot or beaten senseless and left to die. Anyone falling behind in the journey to or from the camp would also be beaten half to death.

The daily regime at Siretz was almost intolerable, but there was yet another chambered bullet in this bizarre game of Ukrainian roulette. If you managed to stay strong enough and fit enough to avoid being weeded out, if you managed to survive the beatings, and if you managed not to break any of the ludicrously arbitrary rules, you could still be a victim. Twice a week, on Friday and Saturday, there were mass executions at the camp. If someone tried to escape, for example, twenty-five prisoners would be shot. They would be chosen at random and Radomsky was always present at the executions. There were also mass executions for whatever were deemed to be serious breaches of camp protocol.

According to a Soviet commission on war crimes, one of the worst single incidents at Siretz came one Sunday in August 1942, not long after the Start players had arrived there. A group of prisoners had taken a momentary pause from a work detail. When one of the local police came to order them back to work he was charged down by a prisoner, who took his gun and shot him dead before making his escape. A senior Gestapo officer arrived from headquarters almost immediately and ordered all of the prisoners to be mustered in front of him. As the prisoners stood there, he announced that eighteen prisoners were going to be shot, in addition anyone who moved in the ranks while this was taking place would also be shot. The exhausted men struggled to stay in line in the burning August heat while the others who were in the working group from which the prisoner had escaped were paraded in front of them. Eighteen men were made to kneel down and the Gestapo chief and his adjutant walked along the line dispatching each man with a bullet in the back of the head. The chief then ordered the camp doctor to bring him all of the sick people in Siretz. Thirty of them were dragged from the bunker and made to kneel down next to the bodies of the first group of men. Again the Gestapo walked along behind them as they faced the massed ranks of the prisoners and shot them all.

After the prisoners had been killed, another detail was ordered to take their bodies to Babi Yar and throw them into the ravine with the thousands of others who had already died there. This was Siretz, Hell on earth. This was the place to which ten footballers had been condemned for their impudent victory in the hot summer of 1942.

# CHAPTER THIRTEEN

Babi Yar was a ravine which had marked the natural boundary of Kiev during the great days of the Kievan Rus. As the furthest outpost of the city there were guards stationed there to watch the road to the north-west and south-east and alert the citizens to any potential attacks. It was a tedious and lonely posting which was only enlivened by the conjugal visits from the wives and sweethearts of the men stationed there. Together they would slip off into the shelter of the ravine and since 'babi' means 'woman's' or 'women's' this is how it came to acquire its name Babi Yar – the ravine of the women.

From 29 September 1941, when the first of the massacres of the Jews had taken place here, the name had lost whatever romantic connotations it might once have had. Babi Yar was now indissolubly linked with death and the prisoners from Siretz were inextricably linked to it. When they died their bodies would be thrown into it, but before they died they had the macabre duty of burying their friends and fellow prisoners after the mass executions. Wholesale slaughter had become a feature at Babi Yar. It had begun with the march of 33,771 Jews from the city in their straggling columns at the end of September 1941. Over two days they were systematically butchered without a single survivor.

A Soviet commission, set up very soon after hostilities ceased to investigate what had happened under the Germans, was given ample evidence by those who lived nearby of what they had seen going on there. The infamous Sonderkommando 4a had carried out the murders, aided and abetted by two battalions of local police.

One witness, a woman listed as S. B. Berlyand, told the tribunal how she had seen forty lorries arrive at Babi Yar on a single day in September. Each lorry was full of men, women and children; all of them were Jewish. Some of the children were no more than babies in arms carried by their anxious mothers. The witness reported:

Along with some other people, I approached Babi Yar without being seen by the German troops. I saw that about fifteen metres from where Babi Yar started, the Germans ordered the Jews to take their clothes off and to start running along the Yar, shooting them from machine guns. I personally saw how Germans were throwing babies into the Yar. There were not only those who were shot dead but also those who were injured and some who remained alive. Nevertheless the Germans started covering them with earth and you could see how certain areas of the ground were moving because there were people still alive under it. Many people, feeling that they were going to die, were fainting, and tearing their clothes off, tearing their hair out and kneeling down in front of the Germans, but they were only beaten with sticks. The execution of the Jews carried on for several days.

Another woman, Ya. A. Steyuk, told the tribunal what she had seen when she found herself in the forest close to the Siretz death camp. She saw that the prisoners, officers and soldiers alike, were indistinguishable from each other because they had no proper clothing and most of them were barefoot. She continued:

Many were in chains. Several of them were shackled together, with a set distance between them so that they could work. In the winter of 1942, I do not remember what month exactly, the Germans brought sixty-five sailors to Babi Yar. Their hands and legs were chained so that they could hardly move and they were absolutely without any clothes and shoes and walking through the snow. It was very frosty. The locals started throwing shoes and shirts to them, but they refused to take them. I remember one of them saying 'We will die for our motherland.' After that they started singing the International and the Germans started beating them with sticks. We knew that they were sailors because they wore their sailors' caps.

The execution of the Russian sailors at Babi Yar is another significant indicator of how the mood in the city of Kiev had changed. When the Germans had taken over the city, the locals had been afraid to set foot out of doors for fear of what might happen to them. Now they had grown in confidence. They were openly defying the Germans by shouting encouragement to these desperate condemned men. The treatment of the Soviet sailors was barbaric even by the appalling standards of the time. They were not merely shackled together, they were bound together with barbed wire which ripped and tore at their flesh with every step. When their bodies were discovered later their skeletons were still tied to each other with barbed wire. This atrocity proved to be too much for the people of Kiev as the men were paraded through the streets of their city. They shouted encouragement, they tried to clothe them, they tried to feed them, and all of it in direct defiance of the Germans. The Kievans were beginning to find a voice. Doubtless by the end of 1942, word was reaching Kiev of what was happening elsewhere. The underground may not have been as active in direct sabotage, but it still provided a conduit for information into the city. The citizens of Kiev would have been aware that the Germans were frozen in and almost at the point of surrender at Stalingrad and would have been inspired by the defenders of that city. The incident, in which ordinary Kievans risked their lives in a brave but futile attempt to help condemned Soviet sailors, was indicative of a restoration of confidence, a process which had begun on the football field with the Start players.

In the winter of 1942 the German dreams of their own dachas by the Black Sea were in total disarray. Now it was Hitler who was ordering his troops to stand and fight to the last man as the Soviet counter-offensive began to roll back the Eastern Front. The 6th Army had surrounded Stalingrad on 6 September, but despite the city having been razed by German bombing raids, the Germans could not cross the Volga to secure a bridgehead large enough to take it. There were 300,000 German troops committed to the battle, but the Soviets fought for every foot of the city. The Red Army had been ordered not to retreat. There is no land beyond the Volga, they had been told. They stood and fought and died to keep the 6th Army at bay. Vasily Chuikov was the Soviet commander of the 62nd Army at Stalingrad. He was a strict, often brutal, disciplinarian, but his strength of will and his uncompromising tactics saved the city. He turned the defenders of Stalingrad into 'living concrete' which spread into every corner of every building. The hand-to-hand fighting was of unimaginable ferocity as the defenders of Stalingrad fought house by house. In the end, after six months of battle, it was the German 6th Army which was itself encircled and its troops who were left in disarray, many of their senior officers having shot themselves through shame or fear of being taken prisoner. Stalingrad had not fallen and if it had not fallen then the Motherland could survive. As the war on the Eastern Front turned against them, the Germans became more and more savage in their treatment of the prisoners in their camps. In fear and desperation they stepped up their efforts at extermination.

In Siretz the Germans had built a special stove for burning partisans, communists and other Soviet activists, according to one tribunal witness. This special stove was used to burn people alive. Those who lived near the camp could hear the awful screams of people as they were forced into the furnace; some who lived nearby could even see the horror from their windows. The witness continued:

In the spring of 1943, I saw how the Germans brought four lorries with civilians to Babi Yar. These people, according to the locals, were brought from the place where the Germans caught the partisans and they were also burned alive. Before doing it, the Germans told them to take their clothes off and then they started pushing them into the stove. I saw how a woman who was passing by the camp threw a piece of bread to the POWs and the Germans shot her immediately.

As the extermination programme was accelerated, every extra day that anyone survived at Siretz became more and more of a victory. The Start players attempted to stay together as much as they could, even though they were on separate work details and fraternising was difficult. Trusevich was the key. He was the one who would pass on messages, restore flagging morale, offer a word of comfort or encouragement to keep his team-mates going. Apart from their higher fitness levels coming into the camp, the Start players had one other advantage which improved their survival chances. They had a reason to survive.

The Jews who were persecuted and died in the camps were there for no other reason than the fact that they were Jewish. Communists on the other hand were there because they were ideologically opposed to Hitler and knew exactly what it meant to oppose Fascism. The Jews were victims, the communists were antagonists. The

Start players were communists and they were also a team. They had agreed to play football in the first place because it offered a way of continuing their fight against the Germans. They had fought for each other outside the camp and they would continue to support each other inside the camp as well. They would have been heartened by the news filtering into the camp about Stalingrad. For some of them there was also the thought that, if Stalingrad still stood and Russia could turn the tide, then they might one day be reunited with the families they had managed to get to safety. The other side of this argument must also have applied. While the men in the camps would have taken solace in the safety of their families, those very families, who must have known what conditions in the camps were like, would have been constantly tormented by the thought of their loved ones being held in such barbaric circumstances.

But in spite of even the most stoically impressive resolve, survival for the Start players was becoming more and more difficult. As post-war testimony suggests, the partisans played a key role in the almost guerrilla-style nature of the Soviet fightback. But every time the partisans struck, the Germans took reprisals. With each attack there were more and more people killed in acts of ever-increasing savagery.

In 1992, Makar Goncharenko reported:

At the beginning of 1943, when the situation at the front changed and resistance in Kiev started going up, executions became more common. Basically anyone who was not serving the occupants could be shot or sent to Germany for work. Each time the partisans became more active, there were more people shot in the Siretz camp . . . The closer the Soviet front got to the Dnieper, the more severe and pointless the executions became. They were just killing prisoners without thinking. One main directive from Hitler in 1943 said that every weak and untrustworthy person should be dead – he was referring to the people of Kiev – and all the rest should be evacuated to Germany. Every third citizen was killed during the occupation, but if you add those who died of starvation or did not come back from slavery in Germany, and those who died during the fighting, basically every second person died. With these statistics it is actually surprising that some of those who were in the Siretz camp managed to survive. Only Komarov and his like were allowed to escape.

Goncharenko made some serious allegations about his team-mate Pavel Komarov. Although he was a prolific goal scorer Komarov had never really fitted in with the rest of the team and there had been shades of opinion about his level of commitment. According to Goncharenko, Komarov had turned traitor in the camp. Given the conditions in which they were trying to survive, it is not difficult to believe that someone would have cracked and offered information to the Germans for relief from the nightmarish routine. If Goncharenko's accusation is true, and there is anecdotal evidence to support the idea of a traitor in the Start ranks, it is possible that Komarov had been supplying the Germans with information even before that. He may have told them about Korotkykh. It does seem that Komarov had agreed to help the Germans by informing on his fellow inmates and in return he was allowed to escape as the Soviet troops advanced towards Kiev. Certainly after the war ended he was never heard from again.

The communist calendar is full of anniversaries of the Revolution and 23 February is one of the most important days in the year. It marks the day when the Red Army was formed and is usually a national holiday and day of celebration. After the dispirited remnants of the German army had finally surrendered at Stalingrad on 31 January 1943, 23 February took on a huge propaganda significance with the partisans staging a number of raids on key targets across the occupied territories. One of these raids was on a plant in Kiev to which the Germans had brought more than a hundred motorised sleighs to be repaired. These sleighs were vital because they were among the few reliable forms of transport in the harsh winter climate. The plant was set on fire by partisans and most of the main work buildings were destroyed along with the storage sheds which held the much-needed sleighs. The following morning, Radomsky ordered a roll-call at Siretz camp.

Word of the partisan sabotage had already reached the camp and the inmates were prepared for the worst. As soon as the alarm was sounded for them to gather in the courtyard the prisoners knew that this was the prelude to yet another mass execution. Radomsky's rage would be almost uncontrollable. The prisoners raced, stumbled and staggered into formation, jostling each other for position. Anyone who was late or deemed to be malingering as the prisoners were assembled could be summarily beaten or shot. Once they had gathered, usually as they stood in their unsteady rows the prison guards walked behind them, between the ranks of prisoners. At intervals a guard would stop behind a prisoner and then either with a club or a rifle butt beat the luckless man to the ground. Another soldier then stepped up and shot the prisoner in the back of the head as he lay senseless and stunned in the dirt.

On the morning of 24 February 1943, the day after the arson attack, Radomsky had decided that every third man was to be shot. The prisoners did not know this, they knew only that there would be reprisals. The guards moved along the lines of men as the anxious prisoners waited and counted. Other than the sound of the jackboots on the frozen earth there was silence. The guards began walking and counting and the shots started to ring out. As the pattern was repeated the prisoners realised what form the reprisal would take; a third of them would die here on the parade ground. It was freezing, they were dressed in rags, but they were too terrified to be aware of the biting cold. As the slaughter went on a guard stopped behind Ivan Kuzmenko. He was by this stage a shadow of the giant who had led the line for Dynamo Kiev and Start, but he still did not give up easily. He knew the moment the soldier's footsteps stopped behind him that he had been marked for death. The guard crashed the butt of his rifle between Kuzmenko's shoulder-blades. He lurched forward but did not fall. The guard hit him again and again. It took several blows of the rifle butt before a near-senseless Vanya was bludgeoned to the ground. The moment he hit the ground another German stepped forward and killed him with a single shot to the back of the head. Further down the line they stopped behind Alexei Klimenko, the youngest and brightest of the Start players. The defender had emerged as one of the stars of the Start side, even the newspapers who were supposed to be hostile to the team recognised his talent. His greatest moment had come when he humiliated the Germans by spurning the chance to score against them. A blow in the small of the back from a rifle sent the slightly-built Klimenko sprawling. One bullet behind the ear and he too was gone. No one dared to turn and see the progress of the executions, anyone who looked round would simply have been shot on the spot, third man or not. Each prisoner strained to listen for the footsteps behind him. Would the footsteps stop or would they move on? They tried to calculate whether they were third in line or whether it would be the man on their right or left. Nikolai Trusevich listened as keenly and desperately as anyone else to the footsteps crunching through the snow and ice. He would not have known that Vanya and Sasha were already among those lying dead on the frost-hardened ground. The footsteps halted right behind him. He was braced for the blow, but it still knocked him to the ground. The agility which had made him the greatest goalkeeper in the Soviet Union brought him straight back up. A prisoner standing close to him in the assembly remembers Trusevich springing to his feet almost instantly. As he jumped up he shouted 'Krasny sport ne umriot' – 'Red Sport will never die' – as the German guard opened fire. Nikolai Trusevich died on his feet wearing his familiar black and red jersey. It was the goalkeeping top he had worn with pride and distinction, it was also the only warm clothing he owned.

The surviving Start players were stunned at the loss of their team-mates. It was not just that they had lost friends, it was also that these three men were among the most ardent and committed members of the team. Without them, especially Trusevich, Bakery no. 3 would probably never have raised a team at all. The tragic news was broken to Makar Goncharenko by Fyodor Tyutchev, one of the oldest men in the Start side. Goncharenko appears to have been planning an escape for some time and had managed to get himself into a position where he was allowed to work outside the main confines of the camp. He was with Sviridovsky in the police station at 48 Melnikova Street. Sviridovsky was a skilled cobbler and was working at the police station repairing boots. Goncharenko had prevailed on him to take him along. Goncharenko recalled:

Sviridovsky was very good at mending boots and in order to escape from the camp I lied that I could do it as well. Mischa taught me very quickly and I was able to convince them that I was a shoe repairer. We found out about the shootings of the other players from Fedya. One of the Germans, a man from a supply unit, had become friendly with him for some reason. He started sending Fyodor out to do harvesting, which was a very privileged thing to do. Fedya knew where we were, and our room faced the street, so he would persuade the coachman to stop for a while and he would then tell us everything that had been happening at the camp.

One of the things which Tyutchev told Goncharenko on the morning after the shootings was that the Germans were looking for him as well. The guards were shooting everyone they could find for the smallest infraction of the rules. Goncharenko and Sviridovsky decided they could not afford to wait around to be found. Goncharenko went on:

> After Fedya's warning we decided to escape. We were locked up for the night by the police. We slept in a cellar which also doubled as the boiler room. Mischa and I slept there on the third tier of the plank beds. We had to use the third tier because the other two tiers were occupied by rats. That night we did not sleep, we stayed awake the whole night talking about escape. We knew that we had been there so long that the policemen had become used to us coming and going. They did not really pay too much attention to what was going on so, in the morning, when we saw a moment we just ran out of the door and kept going. We got to Bohdan Khmelnytsky Square, then we found ourselves in Podol and we managed to lose the police in the lanes there. Sviridovsky went to some relatives and I went to stay with my ex-mother-in-law. She told me that the Germans would come straight to her if they were looking for me, so she managed to persuade some neighbours to take me in.

Goncharenko knew he was taking a risk by staying with the neighbours. They could still inform on him as Korotkykh's own sister had done. But he remained there, safe, until Kiev was liberated.

After Trusevich, Kuzmenko and Klimenko had been shot their bodies were thrown with all the others into the ravine at Babi Yar and crudely buried. Even in death there was one final indignity to be heaped on them. In August 1943, when they knew that the massed Soviet armies on the left bank of the Dnieper were only weeks away from retaking the city, the Germans tried to destroy the evidence of what they had done at Babi Yar. They took more than a hundred prisoners and told them they had to dig up the bodies buried in Babi Yar and burn them. Three Russian Jews who escaped from a firing squad at Babi Yar – L. K. Ostrovsky, V. Yu. Davydov and I. M. Brodsky – recounted an appalling tale to the war crimes commission. The Germans had first gone to the cemetery and appropriated marble headstones and metal fencing for the grisly task. The headstones were put on the ground by their dozens to make a smooth surface and some rails were placed on top. Then the fencing was laid across the rails and firewood was piled on top of the metal fences. The prisoners were then ordered to put a layer of bodies on top of the firewood. Before they were burned another team took earrings, jewellery and gold teeth from the bodies. By alternating layers of kindling with layers of dead a macabre bonfire soon took shape. Once it had reached the required height, gallons of kerosene were poured over this obscene pyre and it was set alight. When the fire had burned down low enough, prisoners were ordered to smash the remaining bones and scatter them and the ashes around Babi Yar. Eyewitnesses among the prisoners who had been forced to carry out the work estimate that around 3,000 bodies were burned at a time.

Even at this rate of incineration the Germans were not content and they ordered an excavator to be brought in so the dead could be piled higher more quickly. From the middle of August until the end of September the work went on for more than twelve hours a day. It is estimated that about 70,000 bodies in all were burned and these included people who were still being killed in the camps while the cover-up was taking place.

By the end of September 1943, the Soviet tanks were at Smolensk to the south of Kiev and the German army was in a state of total disarray. The Soviets took Smolensk and the shell-shocked German troops were now retreating back on Kiev, facing attacks on several fronts as the Red Army moved inexorably forward to reclaim its territory. Just as Stalin had been told in 1941, now Hitler was told two years later that Kiev could not be held and like Stalin he was not disposed to listen to good advice. The Germans had lost vital rail links to the west of the city and the military commander, Field Marshal von Manstein, had begged Hitler to authorise reinforcements. When they finally arrived they were too little and too late, just as von Manstein had been himself when his relief column never got closer than fifty kilometres to the beleaguered Field Marshal von Paulus at Stalingrad. Without the rail links they could not be properly deployed and there was now no alternative but to fall back and surrender Kiev. Again as the Soviets had done in the summer of Operation Barbarossa, von Manstein ordered a scorched earth policy and everything which was deemed to be of use to the attackers was either burned or blown up.

The capture of Kiev was of immense value to Stalin

both in strategic and propaganda terms. When his armies had reached the banks of the Dnieper, north of Kiev, Stalin announced that the first man to cross the river would be awarded the title of Hero of the Soviet Union. This was the highest of honours and it was just the right incentive for the Soviet troops intoxicated by the prospect of reversing one of their greatest defeats. Over the next few weeks, dozens of fanatical communists made the attempt to cross the river. Some tried individually, some in groups. Their persistent efforts meant that before too long between thirty and forty small but significant Soviet bridgeheads had been established on the Kiev side of the river. The Soviets fought tenaciously to hang on to these tiny pockets within the German lines and the Germans wasted a huge amount of time and men bottling up the Red Army in these small enclaves. Von Manstein was convinced that the final push towards Kiev would come from one of the bridgeheads to the south of the city because there it was drier and firmer than the swamps and marshes of the north. However, in the north, one single division of infantry had managed to plough and slither its way through the difficult headlands of the Dnieper. Von Manstein and his officers ignored them because the swamp between them and the city was deemed impassable. It was a fatal mistake which did not allow for the Soviet determination to sweep the forces of the Reich from their country as a prelude to destroying them entirely. While the Germans concentrated on the other bridgeheads, the Soviets secretly reinforced their northern contingent. They were able to get their tanks across the river because the tank crews were so fiercely determined to succeed that they had sealed up every opening in the machines with mud and risked horrible death through suffocation or drowning to drive their tanks virtually underwater to cross the marsh. With their tanks across, the Soviets then surreptitiously moved in other troops to support them, taking advantage of the bad weather which kept the German spotter planes on the ground.

On 3 November 1943, two complete Soviet armies roared out of the north and swept down on Kiev. The panic-stricken German troops, who were gathered on the eastern bank of the river, broke and ran. Many of them were so terrified of what they had heard about the Russian troops and their treatment of captured Germans that they ran headlong into the Dnieper. The river was too wide to swim in full pack and it was too cold for them to stand any realistic chance of survival. They knew that they would not reach the other side. But they had heard so much about the savagery of the Russian troops that they were willing to drown themselves rather than face the zealots as they reclaimed the Motherland. On 5 November, Soviet troops were back in Kiev, a city which was burning from end to end for the second time in two years. At four o'clock on the morning of 6 November, the city was officially recaptured.

With the capital of the Ukraine now back in Soviet hands there was much cause for celebration. Stalin felt that he had won a great victory and was not slow to realise that the city had been taken in time for the anniversary of the Russian Revolution. In Moscow, Stalin ordered an official fireworks display and spoke about 'the year of the great turning point'. While he was toasting his success in Moscow at an elaborate party thrown by his foreign minister Molotov, pockets of fighting continued in Kiev, where the Red Army was still clearing out the remnants of the retreating Germans.

Before the war began Kiev had a population of just over 400,000 people. The city itself had changed hands five times in twenty-five years. This time, when the fighting finally stopped, there were only 80,000 survivors.

# CHAPTER FOURTEEN

Almost within days of retaking Kiev, the Soviets went to work documenting what had happened in the city under German occupation. They wanted the information for two reasons. First, there was the obvious propaganda value, but there was also a sense that they wanted to record what had gone on to prove to their own citizens, especially those in areas such as the Ukraine, that life under the Germans had been grotesquely worse than life under Stalin. The incoming Soviet troops found many photographs of Paul Radomsky scattered in the streets. These pictures, once given to his loyal acolytes, lay abandoned by those self-same henchmen who sought to remove any trace of a link with Radomsky. Information about Siretz and conditions in occupied Kiev was gathered by various Soviet tribunals which began sitting before the end of November 1943, less than three weeks after the city was back in Soviet hands. The key witnesses were a handful of people who had escaped from a shooting squad at Babi Yar in September 1943. It was undoubtedly also through these hearings that the first news of the match between Start and Flakelf – a game which came to be known as 'the Death Match' – began to leak out.

By the end of 1943, news of the game had reached the frontline Soviet troops, who were still fighting the Germans as they continued their push to regain the territory lost to the Axis powers. Opinion at the front differed sharply from the feelings in Kiev. The people who had lived the 778 days under German occupation could not fail to be impressed by how courageous their players had been. There was a time when they were afraid to set foot outside their own doors because of the harsh regime which had been imposed upon them, but to people like this the players from Dynamo and Lokomotiv were real heroes. They also inspired the locals to many other small acts of heroism. Once the Soviets came back to Kiev they found artwork which had been hidden, icons which had been saved, Jews who had been sheltered from the Germans, and heard of others who had been smuggled to safety. But to some soldiers at the front, who had little knowledge of the circumstances in which the footballers had found themselves, the Start players were little more than collaborators.

A famous Soviet athlete, Piotr Dinisenka, who was in the thick of the Soviet counter-attack, summed up the views of many who were actively pressing the war towards Berlin. He wrote when he heard news of the games:

While many thousands of my comrades are hungry and cold, and sitting wet in dirty trenches under Fascist bullets, somewhere my fellow countrymen, in a place far from the front, young and healthy lads, are playing football. They are playing with those who occupied our land and who have tried to eliminate and kill me and against whom I am fighting in inhuman conditions. I am sorry but how do you think I should feel about this, you do not expect me to applaud it?

The problem with the story of Start immediately after the liberation of Kiev was that very few people outside the city witnessed events or knew of them from first-hand testimony. In the months and years after the war, there was a certain prejudice throughout the Soviet Union against people who had lived under German occupation or who had gone to Germany to work. They were marginalised; it was difficult for them to find work and to take their place in mainstream society. But at the same time many of these people were the ones who had actually witnessed the Start games and knew the precise circumstances in which they were played. Since their contributions were effectively excluded, the story began to be distorted and mythic dimensions began to be attributed to it. Eventually the legend of the Death Match emerged.

According to legend, brave Dynamo players fought courageously against the German invaders, but were unable to avoid being caught in the city. Their love of football was so great that even living under the oppressive yoke of the Nazis could not stop them playing the beautiful game. All eleven of them were put into the same factory and played whenever they could. They were so good that not only did their fellow workers forget the war, even the Germans were entranced by their skills.

So entranced in fact that they offered them a place to play, even offering a team to play against them. On the day of the game the stadium was full with more Ukrainians than Germans. It was a carnival atmosphere and Start – the name that the Kiev players had taken – won easily. The Germans were very unhappy and they asked for another game. They also warned the Start players that although they had done well they should remember who was in charge and that things would go badly if they won again. The second match was played the following day. This time the Germans were much less pleasant and fouled the Start players at every opportunity. The referee looked the other way every time. Nonetheless, the Kiev players refused to be intimidated. Despite hunger and near exhaustion they played better than ever and won the match 4–2. The referee blew for full time early and the crowd went wild. As the Start players were leaving the field they were seized by local police, bundled into a truck, and driven to Babi Yar where they were shot still in their strips.

Dramatic though this version may be, it neglects a number of vital details, not least that only four of the team were killed and three of those did not die until six months after the game. There is no trace of Iosif Kordik, no mention of the Lokomotiv players, and no mention of the seven other games which Start played that summer. It even gets the match score wrong.

On the other hand, it is a neat shorthand version of the story which is close enough to the generalities of what actually happened to keep the memory of these players alive. As an aside to the legend which sprang up around the Soviet players, the reaction in Germany was quite different. Joseph Goebbels had already seen the effect that a defeat in a football match could have on the country. Hitler was beside himself when his German side was beaten 2–0 by Norway in the 1936 Berlin Olympics – both goals scored by the Semitic-sounding Isaaksen. After another defeat by Sweden around the same time, Goebbels wrote in his diary: '100,000 left the stadium in a depressed state. Winning a match is of more importance to some people than the capture of a town somewhere in the east.'

In the autumn of 1942, with the tide of war beginning to turn against Germany, Goebbels issued a blanket ban on all international games in Germany or the occupied territories. How much of a part the Start games played in this decision we do not know, but it seems reasonable to assume they had a hand in it.

The legend of the heroic Kiev players continued to thrive, but still there was no official Soviet version of what had happened in those games, even though there were a great many people who knew the truth. One of those who obviously knew the full story was Vladimir Klimenko, the eldest of the three Klimenko brothers. Uncle Volodya, as he was known to everyone, had not missed a game. Not long after the city was back in Soviet hands, he wrote a longhand memoir, in pencil, in a notebook about what had happened in those few dramatic weeks. Vladimir Klimenko was one of the unsung heroes of Kiev and, although he never mentioned it himself, he managed to save a Jewish family from the camps during the occupation. He was also apparently wracked with feelings of guilt and inadequacy because, although he saved a Jewish family, he was not able to do anything to help his own brother. In fact, he had been instrumental in getting young Sasha a career as a footballer in the first place. Vladimir dedicated the rest of his life to keeping his brother's memory alive. Every day Vladimir would sit with his notebook on a bench near his pigeon loft in Gorky Street telling the story of Alexei and the others to anyone who would listen.

Eventually there was one official source of information. The man who probably coined the term 'Death Match' was a Soviet journalist and author called Lev Kassil, who wrote about the game in the party newspaper *Iszvestia*. Kassil had studied documents and spoken to a number of people who had seen Start play and had been at the second game against Flakelf. His story was a truthful and accurate account of events, but his article went largely unrecognised. This may have had something to do with the fact that Kassil's own reputation was somewhat tarnished. He had recently had to publicly apologise for inaccuracies in some of his other stories and this one may have been regarded with some scepticism because of that. On the other hand, Kassil may simply have been warned off by the authorities. They knew the precise account themselves, but the legend suited their purposes better. For whatever reason, Lev Kassil wrote only one story about the Death Match and never followed it up.

The first people from outside Kiev to know what had gone on that summer were the army and the intelligence services who poured into the city in the wake of its liberation. They must have heard something about what had been going on because the surviving footballers were among the first to be interrogated. In his memoir the former Kiev goalkeeper Idzkovsky, who had escaped the encirclement, recalls receiving a number of letters from Makar Goncharenko. In these letters, a plainly worried Goncharenko asked his former team-mate to help him sort out what he would only describe as 'certain accusations' which were being made by the Soviet authorities. Idzkovsky guessed, quite rightly, that since he was well respected by the security services Goncharenko was asking for his protection. Idzkovsky assured them that his friend had done nothing untoward and no action was taken. It was during these investigations that Georgi Gavrilenko, a former inmate at Siretz, gave the eyewitness account of the deaths of Trusevich, Kuzmenko and Klimenko. Also during these hearings it appears to have been established that Pavel Komarov had indeed been working with the Germans and had been allowed to escape by them. By the time they had gathered all of the evidence, the security services very quickly had a clear picture of what had gone on in Kiev, in Zenit Stadium, and then finally and fatally at Siretz death camp. They were aware, too, of the legend, but since they knew that the real story was nowhere near as potently simplistic, they decided to leave the talismanic story in public circulation rather than publish an official version.

The man responsible for the suppression of the official report seems to have been Timofei Strokach, who was the Interior Minister for Sport in the Ukraine after the war. Strokach was one of those who in 1941 had fought shoulder to shoulder with the former Dynamo players as they struggled to fill the barges on the Dnieper in a last desperate attempt to save something of their city. No one knew better than Strokach of the calibre and courage of these footballers and he was the one who took the conscious decision not to diminish the legend by publishing the more complicated truth. He was aided by Timofei Malsevich, who was head of the Ukrainian guerrilla movement from 1942 until 1945. While Malsevich was quick to condemn and demand the execution of known collaborators, he also recognised what conditions had been like in Kiev at the time. He understood the risks that the population had taken and valued the role of the Start players in maintaining morale at a time of national crisis. With this background knowledge he had no hesitation in supporting Strokach in his decision. It was a very fine judgement for Strokach to make. On the one hand, he did not want to suppress the legend, which was a fine example of Soviet selflessness and team spirit, but on the other, he did not want to mythologise anyone to the extent that they would become a martyr and individually greater than the team. In the ten years from 1946 until 1956 when he was Minister for the Interior in the Ukraine nothing was allowed to be published officially and the legend survived in the oral tradition. Finally, in 1959, a book called *The Final Duel* was published which told a version of the story which was closer to the legend than the truth. This attracted international interest and the Start players briefly featured in newspapers, magazines and newsreels around the world. Not long afterwards, an enterprising journalist discovered that three of the players had not died until six months after the games. He published his story but by that stage the legend had taken such a firm grip on the Soviet consciousness that his version was quickly dismissed because the facts did not fit with the myth. Another Soviet writer Anatoly Kuznetsov also tried to tell the story in his book *Babi Yar*, but his version draws heavily on the mythology and succeeded only in reinforcing the myth as the 'official' account. It was through this version, which was published internationally, that the story – albeit the wrong one – reached a wider audience beyond the Soviet Union. This version is also the one which has been propagated through other books by Eduardo Galeano and Simon Kuper.

The men who actually played for FC Start were in a difficult position throughout this period. They knew that the legend was a somewhat simplified version of their story and there were those who wanted to set the record straight. Yet still they remained silent and kept their own counsel. It was a subject which was only for discussion among their team-mates and even then only in the most confidential circumstances. Like almost everyone else in the Soviet Union in the sixties and seventies, the footballers lived in dread of the security services, who had made it quite clear that they preferred the official version. The same message was given to any journalist who dug too deep into the records and documents of the time. This official version meant that, even though Timofei Strokach had intended the story to be an exemplary tale of solidarity in the face of appalling odds, the Dynamo players ended up being lionised as individuals. The myth made them heroes and the state heaped honours and rewards on them. They were hailed as sporting superstars wherever they went. But the surviving players did not feel they had done anything particularly heroic; many of them felt they were receiving the praise and plaudits under false pretences. At one ceremony when the survivors of the matches were being given medals, Mikhail Putistin refused to take his. Putistin was then threatened with prison until he accepted and his team-mates were told to keep quiet about the incident. It was only after he died that Vladimir Balakin spoke openly about what had happened to Putistin and attempted to set the record straight. He was helped by Mikhail Sviridovsky, who felt that the story which was being put about was little more than politically motivated propaganda. Sviridovsky tried to tell people what had really happened but he was too afraid to commit anything to writing or to tape. On the other hand, there were those who were keen to preserve the legend. Idzkovsky, for example, reputedly had a photograph, which was taken after the first game against Flakelf, showing the Start players and the Germans standing side by side looking reasonably cordial. He refused to publish the picture because he felt it would ruin a myth which was now believed by thousands of people. The photograph has now disappeared, presumably destroyed.

Only someone who was from the Ukraine or who truly understood the region could really appreciate what the Start players had endured. In the end, their status was confirmed by two Soviet politicians with strong links to the area, Nikita Khrushchev and Leonid Brezhnev. Khrushchev had been appointed First Secretary of the Ukrainian Party organisation in 1938 and had been in charge when the Ukraine fell to the Germans. It was Khrushchev, allegedly, who had finally convinced Stalin in 1941 that Kiev would have to be surrendered. After the Germans had been driven from the Ukraine altogether, in 1944 he was given the job of restoring agricultural production and rebuilding the industrial base. It was Khrushchev who chaired the Soviet investigation into the atrocities at Kiev which had begun within days of the city being retaken. Not only was he responsible for punishing traitors, but as the man who organised the tribunals he was well aware from first-hand evidence of the part that the Start footballers had played in the war effort in Kiev. When he succeeded Stalin in 1953, the Communist Party effectively gave the official seal of approval to the legend of the Death Match. Khrushchev was succeeded by Brezhnev, himself a Ukrainian, and it was Brezhnev who canonised the footballers as heroes of the Soviet Union. It was during his reign, in 1971, that a monument sculpted by I. S. Gorovoi and designed by V. S. Bogdanovsky and I. L. Maslenkov was erected to the players outside the Dynamo Stadium.

There have been persistent attempts, before and since Brezhnev, to discredit the Start players. Some insist that they were not shot for beating the Germans, but for stealing bread from the bakery. From time to time, witnesses are presented to support this view, but since the most credible of them was only five years old at the time of these alleged thefts, the arguments do not really stand up. Trusevich was also accused by another Dynamo player after the war of having been an NKVD informer. With Trusevich dead and unable to defend himself it is an easy allegation to make, but all that can be said now is that it does not have the ring of truth to it. One intriguing theory suggests that the prime movers of the team – Trusevich, Klimenko and Kuzmenko – were among a number of partisan volunteers who agreed to stay behind in Kiev to organise resistance against the Germans. This version perhaps makes them doubly heroic, since they would know that by staying behind in the city they were almost certainly going to their deaths.

Ultimately, it was Makar Goncharenko, the man who had saved his boots because all he wanted to do was play football, who was to stand as a witness and bear testimony to the heroism of the others. He had no axe to grind, he had no political agenda. Goncharenko was the last survivor. The winger, who had played in the 1936 Dynamo silver medal side, died in 1996. He was in his eighties. Fifty years after the summer of FC Start, he gave a long radio interview in which he recalled what had happened to him and his team-mates. Interestingly, the only part of the story on which he seemed to contradict himself was whether or not Nikolai Trusevich, Alexei Klimenko and Vanya Kuzmenko were shot deliberately or whether it was a random reprisal. When he recounted their deaths as a prelude to his own escape, he said that after Fyodor Tyutchev broke the news to him, he and Mikhail Sviridovsky decided to escape because he felt that they would be next. However, later in the interview, he took a different view of the deaths of his comrades. He said of the players' time after the games:

A desperate fight for survival started which ended badly for four players. Unfortunately they did not die because they were great football players, or great Dynamo players, and not even because Korotkykh was working for the NKVD. They died like many other Soviet people because the two totalitarian

229

systems were fighting each other and they were destined to become victims of that grand scale massacre. The death of the Dynamo players is not so very different from many other deaths.

Start was a very convenient toy for the new owners of the city, which they hoped would help them build a myth about the full and happy life of the local population under the new rulers. In reality this toy only seemed to be under control, it had its own character and its own understanding of the rules of the game. There were nine victories in nine games, they scored fifty-six goals and conceded only eleven and it was not a legend, it was true. For those who participated in these games there was no political motivation in all of this. Of course, their opponents were not always as strong as they were but that means they had a temptation to play without trying too hard, just to please the audience. But they overcame that temptation and they tried to leave a great memory of themselves without thinking about the consequences.

Of course, ideological elements kind of appeared in these games a bit later when each victory for Start became a great moral boost to the citizens of Kiev. According to the official version, the team was not allowed to exist any more because they did not follow the rules of the occupation. That is not true, it just stopped being convenient to those who had previously been quite tolerant of its existence during the hot summer of 1942. In those days, people were shot randomly; anyone could be shot, partisans, commissars, Jews, gypsies, saboteurs, thieves. At the beginning of 1943, when the situation at the front changed and resistance in Kiev started going up, executions became more common and basically anyone who was not serving the occupants could be executed or sent to Germany for work.

Goncharenko's interview throws up one of the most intriguing questions of the entire story. Plainly Korotkykh died because he had been an NKVD officer and his own family had turned him in. But what of the others? Did they die, as Goncharenko suggests, as the inevitable clash of two totalitarian systems or did they die, as he seems to suggest at another point in his interview, as an act of deliberate revenge. It is impossible to say with absolute certainty. In a city which was devastated by two scorched earth retreats in two years, whatever documentation may have once existed does not exist any longer.

The myth promulgated by the Soviets plainly suggests that their deaths were an act of vengeance, since in their telling of the story the players are taken from the field and shot in their strips. On the other hand, when you consider the massive death toll in Kiev in those two years under the German occupation, then the likelihood would be that some of the players held under the conditions at Siretz should have perished. But why those particular players? And why almost all at the same time? In a camp controlled by a sadist, why Trusevich, Klimenko and Kuzmenko all at once?

Trusevich was the moral heart of the team, the driving force which held them together, he was also one of the best loved figures in the Soviet Union. Klimenko was another star player; the young defender who had shone in so many games and humiliated the Germans by refusing to score against them, he was also the son of a prominent local family. Kuzmenko was another charismatic figure, a man who had come to symbolise the physical superiority of the Soviet Union. On top of this we must also consider that no matter what he said fifty years later, Makar Goncharenko, a player who was the darling of the crowds as he tormented the opposing defence, felt at the time that he was also marked for execution. The evidence is circumstantial, but it weighs on the side of there having been an element of deliberation in the choice of victims on 24 February 1943. Why they would choose these three and indeed who chose them is a matter for conjecture. All three of them were well known in Siretz and to the people of Kiev. Perhaps with the tide of war turning at Stalingrad, the Germans felt that a blow to the morale of the people of Kiev was in order. Perhaps Radomsky, the Nazi sadist, simply felt that they had gone too far and he acted out of something as pathetically mundane as vicious spite. We will never know for sure. But Makar Goncharenko seems to suggest that, at the end of the day, the reasons for their deaths are irrelevant. The nature of their deaths was, for Goncharenko, of more abiding significance. He said in 1992:

It may sound cynical, but the four who died were lucky because they could do what they loved even in the occupied territory. In front of everyone, both the citizens of Kiev and the German occupants, they could prove what great players they were without being humiliated and without bowing down to anyone.

# CHAPTER FIFTEEN

The war had a far-reaching effect on Dynamo Kiev. Four of their star players were dead, a fifth had escaped with the Germans, never to be seen again, and the remainder of those who had stayed in the city were so physically devastated they were unable to play again. The club had to rebuild with those players who had been fortunate enough to avoid the rigours of the camp, but it was still more than ten years before Dynamo Kiev tasted anything like the success they had enjoyed before the war. The only link to that previous side was the former goalkeeper Anton Idzkovsky, who played a crucial part in the rebuilding process. He was too old to play in the post-war side but he joined the backroom staff and eventually became the team coach. It was under Idzkovsky that Kiev returned to their former glory when they won the USSR Cup for the first time in 1954, beating Zenit of Leningrad 1–0 in the semi-final before trouncing Ararat of Yerevan in the final by the same score. This victory would herald a remarkable run in the USSR Cup by Dynamo Kiev. All told they have won the tournament nine times – including a Soviet record six wins under the guidance of Valery Lobanovsky – playing a total of 166 games and losing only forty-three.

As a player, Valery Lobanovsky was a member of the successful Dynamo Kiev championship squad of 1961. Kiev won their first league title on 17 October 1961, thanks to a goal-less draw against Kharkov at the huge Republican Stadium in Kiev. The draw meant that they could not be caught in the title race and almost 100,000 people were there to see them win the 22nd championship of the Soviet Union. Since then they have gone on to win the title a further twelve times and Lobanovsky has played a significant role in each of them.

As a player Lobanovsky acquired almost cult status, but it was as a coach that he genuinely excelled and it was under his guidance that Dynamo Kiev achieved their greatest period of success. In 1975, they became the first Soviet team to win a European tournament when they took the European Cup-Winners Cup. In the 1974–5 season, Kiev had beaten CSKA of Bulgaria, Eintracht Frankfurt of Germany, Bursaspor of Turkey and PSV Eindhoven of the Netherlands on the way to the final. In that final in Basle, Ferencvaros of Hungary were put to the sword in a 3–0 rout orchestrated on the field by the great Oleg Blokhin, possibly the finest player in the history of Ukrainian football. Blokhin was a superb athlete who was also trusted to implement Lobanovsky's tactical genius on the pitch. There was still more glory ahead for Blokhin and his finest moments came the following season when, as winners of the European Cup-Winners Cup, Dynamo Kiev took on Bayern Munich, who were the reigning European champions, in the UEFA Super Cup. This was the great Bayern side led by the legendary Franz Beckenbauer, but Kiev beat them 1–0 in Munich and 3–0 in Kiev. Even the German press were unrestrained in their enthusiasm for Blokhin, who was later named European Footballer of the Year.

Dynamo Kiev could reasonably claim to be the best club side in Europe at this stage and, although they were not tested further, you could make a case for suggesting they were the best club side in the world. Ten years of domestic success followed, culminating in another European Cup-Winners Cup triumph. In the final in Lyons they faced Atletico Madrid of Spain and beat them comprehensively 3–0. Again, ten years after his earlier success, Blokhin was at the heart of the victory, scoring a stunning second goal after a move which involved almost every member of the Kiev team. The pre-eminence of Dynamo Kiev was confirmed two years later when Lobanovsky, who was now coach of the Soviet Union's national side, chose twelve Kiev players for his squad for the 1988 European Championship finals in Germany. The Soviet Union had beaten the Netherlands and England and drawn with Ireland in the group stage, then beaten Italy in the semi-final. In the final they again met the Dutch side from the qualifying group, but this time lost 2–0. Even so this was still a considerable achievement for what was effectively a club side.

Throughout this period of extraordinary success, one thing has remained constant in the lives of Dynamo Kiev players. They cannot spend a day at the club without being reminded of the sacrifice which was made by Nikolai Korotkykh, Nikolai Trusevich, Ivan Kuzmenko and Alexei Klimenko. Their presence is constant at the club. They are not at the huge Republican Stadium where 100,000 fanatical Kievans will cram in to watch Champions' League games or the big international fixtures. These four in the shape of their monument keep a watchful eye on the smaller Dynamo Stadium, where Dynamo Kiev goes about the bread and butter business of winning championships in front of 15,000 no less ardent fans. This is where the club conducts its daily business and this is where their monument is to be found.

It is huge and cut jaggedly from a single block of granite which seems to have exploded from the bowels of the earth and into the air. The four men burst from a recess hollowed into the face of the rock because the stone, it seems, can barely contain them. They are tall and proud and strong, magnificent examples of Soviet physicality. They are wearing football shirts and shorts but their muscles seem to ripple even in the cold stone. As they stand four-square in front of whatever faces them, these unnamed men are linking arms, not affectionately, but as a gesture of comradeship and affirmation. The one on the left of the group looks down, an expression more of regret than sadness on his face. To his left and standing a little above him, is a team-mate looking forward with dignity, his downcast eyes the only betrayal of any emotion. Next to him a third man leans forward almost as though he is being restrained by the linked arms of his comrades. The final figure, the one on the extreme right, is neither bowed nor flinching as he stands square-jawed, his chin slightly elevated, and looking beyond the immediate future and into their destiny. The statue itself stands easily three metres tall, comfortably head and shoulders above the tallest man. The texture is rough-hewn and rugged and speaks mutely but eloquently of courage and heroism and Soviet virility. No one could walk past this sculpture without noticing it or stopping to wonder who these men were and why they had been immortalised in this way.

This monument, with a plaque acknowledging the sacrifice of the four former Dynamo players, is what greets players and fans every time they turn up at the club. In club literature, in local match reports, or in conversations with fans it is obvious that being chosen to play for Dynamo Kiev is more than playing for a football team. The fans' conversations are peppered with stirring phrases, almost martial in tone, which refer to players 'defending the colours' or, in a phrase used by Lobanovsky himself, 'defending the honour of Kiev'. It is a substantial responsibility for anyone to live up to, and it is made all the more awesome by knowing that these men made the ultimate sacrifice for the club. Since the monument was erected the post-war generation of Dynamo Kiev players have shown their respect and gratitude to these men in a simple but touching ceremony. Whenever a Kiev player gets married, after the ceremony, the player and his bride will take some time to slip away and leave their wedding flowers at the foot of the statue in a tribute to the men without whom the club would not have existed. One of those who did so was Sergei Baltacha, a member of the 1986 European Cup-Winners' Cup winning squad and the first Soviet player to be allowed to come and play professional football in Britain. In the tradition of the best Kiev players, Sergei Baltacha was a fan before he became a player. As a teenager he idolised the 1975 European Cup-Winners Cup side and the following year, at the age of eighteen, he joined the club. But even before he became a Dynamo Kiev player, Sergei Baltacha knew about the Death Match. He remembered:

I think it is a story which I always knew, even from when I was little. I have known it for such a long time I do not actually remember when I heard it first. I am sure I heard it as a story, but I know also that I read about those players in books and newspapers. But when I was fourteen I went to the Sports Academy and one of my coaches was a Dynamo player who had played with Lobanovsky, and he told us the story very early on. That is one of the ways in which it is kept alive. When you see the monument, and there are many monuments around Kiev because many, many people died in that period, you cannot help but feel that they gave their lives to save us and you have to respect them for that.

When he was playing at Kiev, Sergei Baltacha also remembers meeting Makar Goncharenko, who tried to live a relatively quiet life after the war.

'He was a very distinguished and very respected old man when I met him,' Sergei recalled. 'I think he remained involved in football in some capacity, but he was a very respectable member of Ukrainian society.'

Sergei Baltacha's son, also Sergei, has followed in his father's footsteps and become a professional footballer. The Baltachas have settled in Scotland where young

Sergei has represented his adopted country at international level. But even though they now live far from Kiev, the younger Baltacha is also aware of the sacrifice of his predecessors.

'When he was only little, before we came to live in Britain, Sergei also went to the Sports Academy,' his father explained. 'Like me, he was told the story at a very early age and I know that he remembers it.'

Depending on the prevailing political climate in the intervening years, the administration at Dynamo Kiev has taken an ambivalent attitude to their deceased players. But no matter what the officials and administrators may think, those who proudly wear the blue and white of Kiev are in no doubt about preserving their legacy. There is, according to Sergei Baltacha, a long tradition among Dynamo Kiev players of honouring those who have defended the colours with distinction. His team of European winners looked up to those who had won the Cup before them, and they in turn looked up to the great side of the sixties in which Lobanovsky shone. The current crop of Kiev stars and former stars such as Shevchenko and Rebrov look up to Baltacha's side. And they are all aware of the debt they owe to the men who played for FC Start in the summer of 1942. They have been an inspiration and an example of how football should be played – in spirit as well as in fact – to the players who followed them. Sergei Baltacha explained:

It's one of the reasons why a team like Dynamo Kiev won everything under Lobanovsky. It's because of the mentality of the players he brought up. Football is a team game, it is not about individuals, and the reason why Dynamo Kiev has been so good is that they play as a team. It does not matter how good any individual is, the team is more important. These men made the ultimate team sacrifice, and we became the best club in Europe because we were a team on the park and off the park as well. They are the best example of what it is about to sacrifice yourself and put everything into the team.

# SOURCES

As well as archive documents and contemporary issues of *Nova Ukrainski Slovo*, the following books and newspaper articles were used to provide background material for this book.

Anthony Beevor, *Stalingrad*, Viking, 1998

Alan Clark, *Barbarossa*, Phoenix, 1996

L. P. Franchuk, compiler, *Goalkeeper's Area*, Molod, 1985

Jonathan Glover, *Humanity*, Jonathan Cape, 1999

G. Ye. Kuzmin, *All Secrets Except One*, serialised in *Kyievskiye Novosti* (Kiev News), September–December 1992

James Lucas, *War on the Eastern Front*, Greenhill Books, 1998

Vladimir Mayevsky, 'Ivanov, who Saw the Death Match', *Zerkale Nedell* (Weekly Mirror), 30 August 1997

V. I. Mirsky and B. A. Semibarsky, *Attacking Heights*,
Zderovye, 1980

Brian Moynahan, *The Russian Century*, Pimlico, 1997

Richard Overy, *Russia's War*, Allen Lane, 1997

Laurence Rees, *War of the Century*, BBC Books, 1999

Anna Reid, *Borderland*, Phoenix,1998

James Riordan, *Sport in Soviet Society*, Cambridge
University Press, 1977

P. Severov and N. Khalemsky, *The Final Duel*,
Fizcultura, 1959


I have also drawn on the testimony of the following
witnesses contained in the report *Mass Annihilation of
Peaceful Citizens and Soviet POWs.*

S. B Berlyand
I. M. Brodsky
V. Yu. Davydov
L. K. Ostrovsky
Ya. A. Steyuk

All Fourth Estate books are available from
your local bookshop

Or visit the Fourth Estate website at:

# www.4thestate.co.uk